Anwar Sadat and Menachem Begin

Negotiating Peace in the Middle East

MODERN PEACEMAKERS

Modern Peacemakers

Anwar Sadat and Menachem Begin

Negotiating Peace in the Middle East

Heather Lehr Wagner

CHELSEA HOUSE
PUBLISHERS
An imprint of Infobase Publishing

Anwar Sadat and Menachem Begin

Chelsea House
An imprint of Infobase Publishing
132 West 31st Street
New York NY 10001

ISBN-10: 0-7910-9000-0
ISBN-13: 978-0-7910-9000-8

Library of Congress Cataloging-in-Publication Data
Wagner, Heather Lehr.
  Anwar Sadat and Menachem Begin: negotiating peace in the Middle East / Heather Lehr Wagner.
      p. cm. — (Modern peacemakers)
  Includes bibliographical references and index.
  ISBN 0-7910-9000-0 (hardcover)
  1. Israel–Arab War, 1973—Juvenile literature. 2. Sadat, Anwar, 1918-1981—Juvenile literature. 3. Begin, Menachem, 1913-1992—Juvenile literature. 4. Arab–Israeli conflict 1993—Peace—Juvenile literature. I. Title. II. Series.
  DS128.115.W34 2007
  956.04'8—dc22   2006028382

Text design by Annie O'Donnell
Cover design by Takeshi Takahashi

Printed in the United States of America

Bang FOF 10 9 8 7 6 5 4 3 2 1

This book is printed on acid-free paper.

All links and Web addresses were checked and verified to be correct at the time of publication. Because of the dynamic nature of the Web, some addresses and links may have changed since publication and may no longer be valid.

TABLE OF CONTENTS

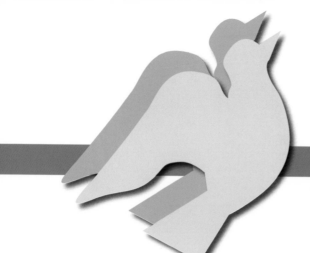

CHAPTER 1

The October War

Early in the afternoon of October 6, 1973, Egypt and Syria launched near-simultaneous attacks on Israeli-held territory. It was Yom Kippur, the holy Day of Atonement in the Jewish calendar. It was also the tenth day of Ramadan, a period of fasting and prayer for Muslims. The attacks initiated what would come to be known as the October War.

The first attacks came from Egyptian troops, who launched an artillery barrage against Israeli forces on the eastern bank of the Suez Canal. Egyptian missiles provided air cover, while high-pressure hoses drilled holes in the sand barriers Israeli forces had constructed. Once the holes were large enough, Egyptian armored tanks and vehicles moved through on temporary bridges. The Israeli troops were unprepared for the attack, and by midnight, nearly 80,000 Egyptian troops crossed the Suez and were positioned inside the Israeli fortifications.[1]

At nearly the same time, Syrian troops moved south and attacked Israeli forces on the Golan Heights. Israelis in the northern and southern regions of the Golan Heights provided fierce resistance, but Syrian tanks were able to advance more easily in the southern por-

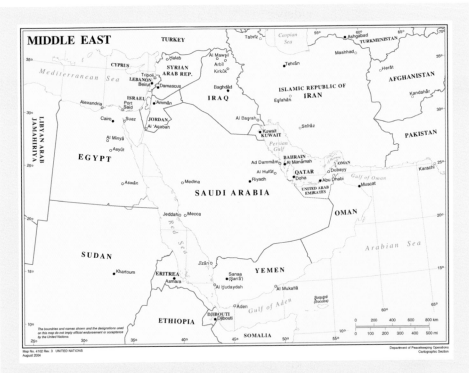

National boundaries in the Middle East shifted many times during the twentieth century. The map above shows the geography of the region as it was in 2004.

tion of the territory, and troops reached the Jordan River within 24 hours.

Israel's prime minister, Golda Meir, had received intelligence that Syrian and Egyptian troops were conducting military drills along the Israeli borders in May 1973. These observations suggested that the exercises seemed to involve large numbers of soldiers. In addition, the Egyptian president, Anwar Sadat, had publicly announced his intention to take military action against Israel in the near future. Sadat, however, had already threatened Israel multiple times without following up on the threats. Israel had successfully resisted previous attacks from Arab nations; in fact, its territory had increased dramatically with each successive war. Based on the evidence and their assessment of Egypt's military capabilities, Israeli intelligence experts concluded that Sadat was bluffing once again.

Ultimately, the intelligence experts were mistaken, and the Golan Heights and Suez Canal became symbolic, as well as military, targets. The Gaza and Sinai territories leading to the Suez Canal had been seized from Egypt by Israeli troops during the Six Day War in June 1967. In that same conflict, Israeli troops had captured Syrian territory in the Golan Heights.

Six years after that bloody conflict, Syrian and Egyptian leaders had grown weary of waiting for diplomatic measures to force Israel from these occupied territories, and they were determined to take the land by force.

A QUESTION OF HONOR

Israeli forces were caught by surprise in the initial hours of the attack, but they quickly rallied. Within a week, Israeli troops were mounting strong counterattacks against both the Syrian and Egyptian troops. By October 25, Syrian troops had been pushed back across the 1967 cease-fire line into Syrian territory, and Egyptian troops were engaged in fierce combat with Israeli forces along the Suez Canal.

Two allies of the fighting nations became involved in the conflict. The Soviet Union and the United States were, at the time, the two most powerful nations in the world, and each favored a different outcome. The United States had long been a strong supporter of Israel, whereas the Soviets had assisted both Egypt and Syria with supplies.

The relationship between the Soviet Union and Egypt had grown prickly by the time President Sadat came to power in 1970. He had expelled Soviet advisers who, he believed, were threatening his leadership. In 1973, when the Soviet ambassador attempted to broker a cease-fire shortly after the war began (supposedly at the request of Syria), Sadat rejected the offer.

Golda Meir (above) was the prime minister of Israel from 1969 to 1974. The October War, during which Egyptian and Syrian forces attacked Israel, occurred during her tenure. A year later, Meir resigned from her post.

The Soviet Union did send supplies and equipment to Egypt and Syria. In his memoirs, Sadat charged that it was the involvement of the United States (in supplying tanks, missiles, and ammunition to Israel) that led him to accept a cease-fire. Sadat notified Syria of his decision, declaring, "I put on record, in that telegram, the substance of my stand on this issue." He later wrote, "I was not afraid of a confrontation with Israel but . . . I would not confront the United States. I would not allow the Egyptian forces or Egypt's strategical targets to be destroyed once again."[2]

A cease-fire was tentatively agreed to on October 22, but numerous violations threatened to widen the conflict. Arab nations pledged their support to Egypt and Syria, and the Soviet Union suggested that both the Soviets and the United States should send military contingents to Egypt. American Secretary of State Henry Kissinger was soon involved in "shuttle diplomacy" (a series of quick trips) between Israel, Egypt, and Syria to obtain agreements to end the fighting.

The war officially lasted only 16 days, but its consequences were serious and enduring. Both sides would claim victory in the conflict—the Israelis because their forces had prevailed in the end, and the Egyptians because they had finally proved that the Israeli forces could be defeated. Thousands of soldiers on both sides were killed or wounded. Both sides also suffered tremendous losses in military equipment and supplies. Israel's failure to anticipate the attack would eventually force its prime minister, Golda Meir, and its defense minister, Moshe Dayan, to step down.

When the U.S. airlift of supplies and equipment to Israel became public, a coalition of Arab nations, including Saudi Arabia, responded by instituting an oil embargo on the United States. As oil supplies dwindled and costs skyrocketed, the average American quickly realized that conflict in the Middle East had direct consequences in American cities and towns. Suddenly, more than ever before, peace mattered.

Henry Kissinger is pictured above with President Gerald Ford. As secretary of state under Ford, Kissinger played a significant role in mediating between Israel and Egypt, including overseeing the return of the Suez Canal to Egyptian control.

A SLOW PATH

The oil embargo—the first real test of the value of oil as a political weapon—lasted from October 1973 to November 1974. The results included gasoline shortages and high prices of oil, which hindered the U.S. economy.

U.S. Secretary of State Henry Kissinger accelerated his efforts to encourage limited peace, using a "step-by-step" method rather than attempting to achieve peace in one fell swoop. Eventually, Kissinger's efforts paid off, and a 1974 agreement gave Egypt control of the Suez Canal and Syria control of some of the territory it held before 1967.

As a result of these negotiations, a relationship gradually formed between Sadat and Kissinger, and ties between Egypt and the Soviet Union weakened. Sadat acknowledged in his memoirs, "The U.S. played an important role in the reopening of the Canal." He also wrote, "Rather than acting as a policeman who throws his weight about, the United States stood by me and showed her real face."[3]

The relationship between Egypt and Syria grew cooler. Compromises made by Sadat after the war would be viewed with distaste in Syria, a nation that increasingly allied itself with more militant nations, such as Iraq, Libya, and Yemen.

One of the most significant results of the 1973 war was, arguably, the way in which conflict made peace possible. For the first time, Israel's military power was not overwhelmingly superior to that of its neighbors. It had been able to push back the attack, but not without a painful lesson. For the first time in many years, Egypt had not been forced into a humiliating military defeat, and this newfound strength meant that negotiations could begin. Both sides had suffered great losses, and both sides were ready to take steps to prevent further bloodshed.

Little more than four years after his troops launched a blistering attack against Israel, in 1977, Egyptian President Anwar Sadat traveled to Israel. This official visit was the first made by any Arab leader to Israel since that country had come into existence. Sadat spoke before the Knesset, the Israeli parliament, and outlined his plan for peace.

Israel's new leader, Menachem Begin, responded in kind, visiting Egypt on December 25. Begin became prime minister of Israel in May 1977. He was head of the Likud Party, known for its pledge to retain control of Israeli-held territory in the West Bank and Gaza. Like Sadat, Begin seemed to sense that a historic opportunity existed—an opportunity to bring an end to decades of violence and war.

In September 1978, Menachem Begin and Anwar Sadat traveled to the American presidential retreat, Camp David, for another historic meeting. At the meeting's end, an agreement had been reached to press forward toward a peace treaty with aspirations to full and normal relations between Egypt and Israel. As a result of this meeting, and their bold efforts to move their countries in a new direction toward peace, Menachem Begin and Anwar Sadat were jointly awarded the Nobel Peace Prize in 1978.

The presentation speech was delivered by the Chair of the Norwegian Nobel Committee, Aase Lionaes, on December 10, 1978. In her speech, Lionaes stated factors that led to the Committee's decision to nominate Begin and Sadat for the award:

Camp David

In 1978, Sadat and Begin would come together in a truly historic meeting hosted by U.S. president Jimmy Carter. The location was the presidential retreat known as Camp David, about 70 miles (113 kilometers) from Washington, in the Catoctin Mountains of Maryland.

It was President Franklin D. Roosevelt who first established Camp David on the site of a camp for federal workers and their families. Roosevelt drew up the plans for the construction of a main lodge and improvements to many of the cabins on the grounds; he called it "Shangri-La" and was the first president to use the facility, for a three-day retreat in 1942. He also hosted the first foreign official there—British Prime Minister Winston Churchill, in 1943.

President Dwight Eisenhower renamed the retreat Camp David in honor of his grandson, David Eisenhower. Eisenhower was the first to host a cabinet meeting at Camp David.

President Ronald Reagan spent more time at Camp David than any other president. President George H. W. Bush's daughter, Dorothy, was married there.

In addition to privacy and cooler temperatures, Camp David offers a pool, putting green, driving range, tennis courts, and a workout center. Presidents continue to use Camp David as a site for more informal or private meetings, both with staff and foreign guests. The president normally travels to Camp David by helicopter.

Never has the Prize been closely associated with agreements such as the two Camp David agreements, which provide the basis for the award to the two statesmen on whose shoulders such grave responsibilities have fallen.

Never has the Peace Prize expressed a greater or more audacious hope—a hope of peace for the people of Egypt, for the people of Israel, and for all the peoples of the strife-torn and war-ravaged Middle East.[4]

In his Nobel Lecture, Begin noted the significance of what he and Sadat had undertaken: "In the spirit of the Nobel Prize tradition we gave to each other the most momentous pledge: No more war. No more bloodshed. We shall negotiate and reach agreement."[5]

The peace process initiated by these two men did not lead, as they had hoped, to a more permanent and lasting peace in the Middle East. The conflict that had simmered for decades would spill over again and again. For a brief period of time, however, the picture of two men—whose countries had faced each other on the battlefield five years earlier—clasping hands would resonate around the world. For that moment, peace seemed possible. As Sadat noted in his memoirs, "I believe that for peace a man may, even should, do everything in his power. Nothing in this world could rank higher than peace."[6]

CHAPTER 2

Childhood Under British Occupation

I n a small village named Mit Abul-Kum along the Nile Delta, Anwar
Sadat was born on December 25, 1918. He was one of 13 children.
At the time, Egypt was under British occupation. Anwar's father,
one of the few educated men in the village, was employed as a military hospital clerk. Soon after Anwar's birth, his father was posted
to Sudan, in Africa.

Anwar's mother, a Sudanese immigrant, was illiterate. His
grandmother was also illiterate, but she had great skill as a healer
and was respected in the village for her ability both to cure illnesses
with herbs and to solve personal problems with her wisdom. Young
Anwar adored his grandmother, and his earliest memories involved
accompanying her on walks through the village.

His was a happy, simple childhood. Anwar, dressed in traditional
village clothing—a long robe over a white calico shirt—would go out
at sunrise to take the cattle into the fields or to the canal for water. He
helped work the ox-drawn threshing machine and pick cotton during
the harvesting season. The farmland in the village was rich, and young

Anwar Sadat is shown wearing his naval uniform in this photograph from 1981. Sadat was president of Egypt from 1970 until his death in October 1981.

Anwar picked carrots, onions, or dates for a snack. In the heat of the day, he would rest under a tree. At night, he and the other boys of the village gathered outside to play games in the moonlight.

Water was a precious resource. The canal that supplied water to the village would overflow for no more than two weeks each year. During that time, all the villagers would work cooperatively to ensure that everyone's land was irrigated.

Anwar, however, was not an ordinary village boy. His father had earned the prized General Certificate of Primary Education, and so he was addressed respectfully as *effendi* (the English equivalent would be "sir"). Anwar's grandmother had similar plans for her grandson. He attended the village's Koranic Teaching School, where he memorized passages of the Koran, the holy text for Muslims, and learned to read and write. At this school, each student sat on the floor and held a writing tablet and a pen made from a reed. In his pocket, Anwar kept bread crusts and dry cheese, and he would snack on them throughout the day.

Eventually, Anwar was sent to a Coptic Christian school in Tukh, about a half mile from his village. Each morning, the students would be summoned to class by the ringing of the large school bell.

Anwar did not stay long at the Christian school. The British occupation was weighing heavily on Egyptians, and in 1924, the British commander of the Egyptian Army was assassinated. The British responded by withdrawing the Egyptian Army from Sudan. Anwar's father soon came back to the village, but the family did not remain in Mit Abul-Kum for long. Shortly after his return from the Sudan, Anwar's father announced that the family was moving to Cairo, Egypt's capital city.

STRUGGLES IN THE CITY

Anwar's family moved to Cairo in 1925, when he was almost seven years old. Life in the city was a dramatic change for the young boy. Finances were tight for the family, though, so Anwar's

Two small Egyptian boys tag alongside a patrol of British Paratroopers in a rubble-strewn street in Port Said, Egypt, in 1956. There is a long history of British involvement in Egyptian affairs, whether directly, through military occupation, or indirectly, through commercial relations.

father chose to send him to the Islamic Benevolent Society School, in part because the fees were reasonable.

Each day, as Anwar walked to school, he passed one of the palaces of King Fuad. The palace featured a lavish orchard, with apricot trees that tempted Anwar and his friends. Occasionally in the spring, when the apricots were in season, Anwar and his friends would reach up and pick a few of the precious apricots, even though they knew that to touch anything of the king's could mean a death sentence.

At the age of 12, Anwar received the General Certificate of Primary Education—the same degree that had earned his father great respect. His father was determined that his sons, Anwar and

Tal'at, would continue their education; therefore, the boys were enrolled at the Fuad I Secondary School.

According to Egyptian law at the time, if one brother was enrolled at the expensive private school, then the other should not have to pay tuition. Unfortunately, for unknown reasons, the younger Sadat did not receive the tuition exemption, so his father was forced to pay for both sons. Because of the cost, he was allowed to pay in installments, the first of which equaled an entire month's salary.

With family finances so tight, it was clear that the Sadats could not continue to educate both sons. Luckily for Anwar, after a month, his brother declared that he did not wish to continue his education, so Anwar, the younger of the two, was allowed to remain at the school.

It was at this school that Anwar Sadat first encountered the prejudices and class differences that separated members of Egyptian society. Many of his classmates were wealthier and better dressed than he was, and some looked down on him as a "villager." His village accent caused some to laugh at him. He could only afford a cup of milky tea, whereas his classmates bought chocolate and candy.

British military officers were a constant presence in Cairo. Anwar often found himself longing for his village and for the life he had known there. Each year, when school ended, he returned to Mit Abul-Kum.

Anwar's early school career did not end as his father had hoped. He failed to earn high enough grades to enable him to continue on to higher education. He finally obtained his General Certificate of Education after transferring to several different schools. Sadat later wrote of these trials in his memoirs, noting, "The result was a turning point in my life," and "I realized that my failure was a sign. God was not satisfied with me, perhaps because of my negligence, perhaps because of my overconfidence. To maintain my inner strength, I could do nothing better than turn to the values of our village, as I had always done."[7]

MILITARY CAREER

As a young man, Anwar Sadat began to feel a real sense of admiration for those who dared to challenge the British. When Mohandas Gandhi passed through Egypt on his way to Britain in 1932, Sadat carefully read all accounts of Gandhi's peaceful resistance against the British occupation of India.

Sadat's admiration for Gandhi was so strong that he decided to completely imitate his hero. He stopped wearing clothing and instead covered himself from the waist down with an apron, in imitation of Gandhi's simple form of dress. Because Gandhi was rumored to spin thread for his own clothing with a spindle, Sadat, too, made a spindle and retreated to the roof of the family home. After several days, Sadat's father persuaded him to find other ways to honor Gandhi, noting that in the bitterly cold weather, he was more likely to contract pneumonia than make any difference in Egyptian politics.[8]

World events soon affected Sadat's life path. Hitler was on the march, with an aim to rebuild Germany after its defeat in World War I. Soon, however, the German army would turn its sights on other countries. At the same time, a treaty signed between Egypt and Britain dictated that the Egyptian Army would be allowed to expand. This was a critical development for Sadat. Previously, the Egyptian Army had been small and highly select. Generally, only sons of very wealthy and powerful families were admitted into the military academy. In 1936, however, when Sadat was nearly 18 years old, the rules were changed, so that members of the middle and even lower classes might hope to gain admittance to the military academy.

Sadat, despite the present opportunity, still faced several challenges. On the application, he needed to list his father's income and property. It was also required that he supply an influential reference. At the time, Sadat's father was working as a senior clerk in the Department of Health. He had a fixed income, meaning that Sadat could supply details of this income on his application.

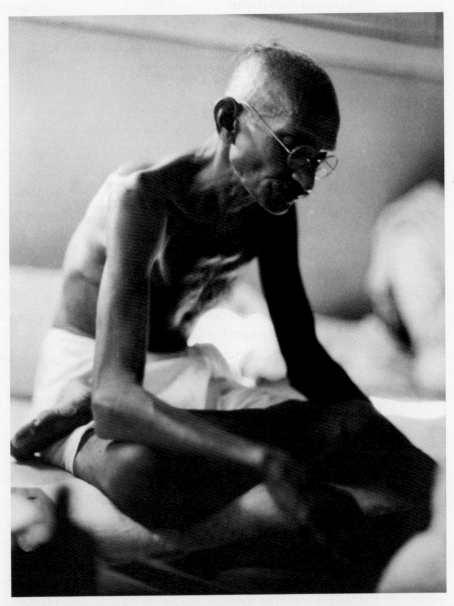

As a young man, Anwar Sadat developed a great admiration for Mohandas Gandhi's peaceful resistance against the British occupation of India. He decided to forgo regular clothing, like his hero, Gandhi. Instead, he covered himself from the waist down with an apron, as Gandhi wears in the photograph above.

The family knew no one powerful and influential enough to serve as a suitable reference, however. Finally, Sadat's father remembered that a friend of his—an officer with whom he had served in Sudan—was working for Major General Ibrahim Khayri Pasha. The major general served as chair of the committee that evaluated the military academy applications; he certainly would be a suitable reference.

The major general lived in a palace in one of Cairo's wealthiest districts. Sadat and his father traveled to the palace one day. At the suggestion of the family friend, the Sadats were to linger in the major general's hallway. When he passed them, he would ask them what they wanted, and they would be given the opportunity to request the reference.

The humiliating encounter that followed would remain with Sadat for the rest of his life. The major general appeared on schedule, noticed them in the hallway, and one of his staff hastily whispered the reason for their presence. The man then looked at Sadat's father and said haughtily, "Oh, yes. You're the senior clerk of the Health Department, and that's your son who . . . I see . . . all right, all right!"[9] He then hurried through the door, mumbling something that neither Sadat nor his father could hear. In the end, he ignored their request.

Ironically, Sadat would encounter the same man about 30 years later. Sadat had become the speaker of the National Assembly, and the major general appeared in his office to request help with some confiscated property and some business involving his sons. Sadat took care of the man's requests, then reminded him of that meeting several decades earlier in which he had ignored the request of the young man whose help he now sought. Sadat reassured him that he held no hard feelings; indeed, he noted that it was because of men like him that the revolution had been possible.[10]

Sadat was forced to find another reference. Finally, the British chief medical officer of the Egyptian Army, under whom his father had worked, agreed to provide one. He provided a detailed recommendation, and although this reference was far less impressive than one from the major general would have been, Sadat was granted admittance to the academy. He was one of 52 accepted that year.

When Sadat went to the military academy to pay his fees for the year, however, he discovered that his acceptance had been withdrawn. The Egyptian minister of war had six relatives whom he wanted to enroll in the military academy. Six places needed to be found for these new cadets, so Sadat's name was struck from the acceptance list. The medical officer who had served as Sadat's reference attempted to intervene. Finally, after the academy had already been in session for 26 days, Sadat was allowed to enroll.

Atatürk

Sadat was greatly inspired by the man who had transformed Turkey from the aging center of a defeated empire into a modern nation. That man was Mustafa Kemal, but it is as Atatürk—"Father Turk"—that he is best known.

The man who would one day be acclaimed as the "Father of all Turks" was born in 1881 to a middle-class Muslim family in the town of Salonica (now in Greece, but at the time part of the Ottoman Empire). His father died when he was only 7; at the age of 12, he enrolled in the military academy. He went on to attend Istanbul's elite War College and pursue a career in the military.

Disenchanted by the corruption of the sultan, the Ottoman ruler, and the poor conditions suffered by those serving in the military, Mustafa Kemal joined with other alienated officers in plotting revolution. He became a military hero in World War I, but when the Ottoman forces were defeated, British troops occupied the Ottoman capital of Istanbul.

Civil war followed, and in the end, both the British and the sultan were forced to leave the country. Mustafa Kemal became Turkey's president and immediately took steps to modernize his nation. He wanted his country to become a republic with a democratically elected national assembly, a

At the academy, Sadat focused on heroic political leaders, such as Mustafa Kemal Atatürk, the great Turkish ruler who had successfully championed a revolution, then transformed his nation into a powerful and modern country. He also studied Egyptian history, familiarizing himself with the events that had led to British occupation in 1882 and what had happened since then.

Soon, Sadat was dreaming of a revolution that would liberate Egypt. He wanted to target both the British and the corrupt Egyptian government that functioned as a puppet of the British regime. Sadat wrote in his memoirs:

truly radical idea in a country that had known centuries of rule by a monarch.

Atatürk promoted greater rights for women, closed religious schools, and closed the courts where law was shaped by the Koran. He outlawed the traditional Turkish head covering—the fez—worn by men, and encouraged women to stop wearing the veil. Instead, both sexes were to adopt Western styles of dress. The Christian calendar was introduced, as was the European concept of the 24-hour measurement of daily time. The phrase in the Turkish Constitution that stated "the religion of the Turkish state is Islam" was removed.

In addition, the Arabic alphabet was eliminated, and the Latin alphabet, the one used in all Western languages, was introduced. Turks needed to relearn to read and write using the new alphabet. By 1935, all Turkish citizens were legally required to take a last name.

This radical reshaping of Turkish society was all intended to place Turkey in a competitive position internationally. Within a relatively short period of time, Atatürk transformed how his people dressed, the alphabet they used to read and write, the clocks and calendar by which they measured time, their laws and system of government, even their names.

Atatürk died of cirrhosis in 1938. He had led Turkey as president for 15 years.

I decided to start with our own position as officers in the Egyptian Army. . . . Since the surest way to a man's heart was to deal with what concerned him personally, I focused in my conversations with my colleagues on two things which, everybody agreed, damaged the army and our life in the armed forces in general. The first was the absolute power of the British military mission; the second, our senior officers' ignorance and blind acquiescence in whatever the British commanded.[11]

Sadat was, at last, a cadet in military school. In order to keep custom, he was married at a young age to a distant relative. He became a father, and eventually, Sadat and his first wife had three children. Despite all these successes, though, Sadat continued to focus his thoughts on revolution.

CHAPTER 3

Boyhood
in Poland

Menachem Begin was not born in a small village, but in Brisk, located in eastern Poland (now it is known as Brest and is part of Belarus). The town would gain international fame near the end of World War I, when representatives from Germany and Russia would meet there to sign a treaty to end the war in the East.

The town had a strong and vibrant Jewish community, which ran high schools as well as medical, cultural, and welfare organizations. Begin's father, Zeev-Dov Begin, was a respected figure in this community. One of nine children of a timber merchant, Zeev-Dov had studied at a Jewish school until the age of 17, when he attempted to run away to study medicine at a university in Berlin. His father caught him at the train station and persuaded him to return home by telling him that his help was needed with the timber business.

Soon afterward, in 1906, Zeev-Dov married Hasia Kosovsky, the daughter of a timber merchant. Menachem Begin was born on August 16, 1913; he was their third child and second son. The name *Menachem* means "consoler" in Hebrew. His godfather was Brisk's chief rabbi. The family lived in a four-room apartment in a wooden house near

Menachem Begin is shown in this photograph from 1972. Begin was born in Brisk, in what was then Poland, in 1913. He immigrated to British-controlled Palestine in 1941, and served as the prime minister of Israel from 1977 to 1983.

the center of town. The house had no running water or electricity, but this was typical of most homes in Brisk at that time.

World War I began shortly after Menachem's birth. By 1915, refugees were coming into Brisk from areas closer to the front. Menachem's father invited the refugees to his home and offered them meals. He welcomed both Russian and Polish refugees, even though his support was firmly on the side of the enemy Germans. His outspoken opinions in support of Germany, and his widely expressed belief (which later proved to be correct) that German forces would soon invade Brisk, caused trouble for Zeev-Dov. Town officials soon asked him to leave, and he was forced to travel to Moscow and then to St. Petersburg, Russia, as the war continued. Menachem's mother was left behind in Brisk with their three children.

The remainder of the Begin family's time in Brisk was brief. The city was evacuated just before German forces invaded. The family traveled by horse-drawn wagon to a cousin's home in a more remote part of Poland. Two days after they fled, the town of Brisk was burned.

Zeev-Dov rejoined his family while they were staying with their cousin, but their sanctuary did not last long. The front soon shifted, and the invading Russian army forced the family from their home and set flames to it.

RETURN TO BRISK

The Begin family moved several times in the ensuing years. Much of Poland was caught between invading German and Russian forces, and the front shifted often. The family stayed with Zeev-Dov's father for a while. After four years of moving from place to place, they were finally able to return to Brisk. Zeev-Dov had been given permission to rebuild the synagogue, a hospital, and several homes.

Menachem attended the Tachkemoni School, a primary Jewish institution. His faith was important to him. He accompanied his father to synagogue on Friday nights, and as a young boy, he earned a reputation for his ability to quote extensive passages of Jewish scripture with skill and passion. At 14, he transferred to a school run by the Polish government. He was one of only three Jewish students in the school, but he made no attempt to hide his faith or his Jewish identity. In one case, he received a failing mark in Latin (a class at which he normally excelled) because the exam was scheduled for a Saturday. When Begin informed his teacher that Saturday was the Jewish Sabbath (or day of rest), his classmates laughed at him. "I might have given in and written the exam," Begin later recalled, "but they laughed, and I wasn't going to let them think that I surrendered because of their laughter."[12]

Prejudice against Jews was simmering beneath the surface in Poland, and Begin was certainly aware of it in his school and in the streets of Brisk. Universities were kept segregated: During lectures, Jewish students were required to sit at the back of the room. In addition, Jewish customers were not welcomed at certain cafes and theaters.

THE RISE OF ZIONISM

Menachem Begin spent his teen years living in a traditional Jewish community. His family was middle-class, and Zeev-Dov had clear aims for his son: He wanted him to become a lawyer.

The Zionist movement was growing in Poland, however, and Brisk was no exception. Zionism began as a political movement in response to growing signs of anti-Semitism in Europe. The movement advocated the creation of a Jewish homeland (in the territory then known as Palestine), where Jews from around the world could build their own state.

As a young man, Begin heard his father speak of this ideal, a return to a homeland. "The day will come when we will all be in the Land of Israel," Zeev-Dov said, inspiring his son with dreams of traveling to that land himself.[13] Begin respected his father deeply; he witnessed his courage when faced with anti-Semitism. A Polish soldier once accosted Zeev-Dov and a rabbi with whom he was walking; pulling out a knife, the soldier threatened to cut off the rabbi's beard. In response, Zeev-Dov took his walking stick and hit the soldier. Both Zeev-Dov and the rabbi were arrested and imprisoned at a military fort, where they were beaten severely.

Begin loved chess and reading, but in 1926, at age 13, he became passionate about Zionism and joined a Zionist youth group called Betar. Many Zionist groups operated in Brisk; some were closely linked to the Communist movement, and others strongly urged their members to prepare for immigration to Palestine. Betar was distinct from many of these—it was a youth group modeled after the ideals of the militant Zeev Jabotinsky and was designed to inspire young Jewish men with the idea of working for the creation of a Jewish state. The Betar movement relied on a more militant approach to Zionism, however. Under Jabotinsky's direction, Betar advocated the creation of a Jewish army to take over Palestine by force. Betar inspired Begin and others with the idea of a nationalism connected to militarism and independence that could only be achieved with military strength.

This concept was radically different from the ideas put forward by some of the more socialist Zionist groups, which were advocating agricultural settlement of Palestine. These groups supported the idea of collective pioneering and farming of unsettled territories in Palestine. These groups intended to build a better society for Jews in their traditional homeland, one acre at a time, encouraging them to return to Palestine to create agricultural settlements in collective farms.

But, Jabotinsky and his followers believed that agricultural settlements would never force the British, who controlled the territory of Palestine after World War I, to provide Jews with a homeland there. Soldiers, they believed, were far more impressive than farmers, and only through the flexing of military muscle would Jews win their homeland.

As part of Betar's military orientation, the movement encouraged parades, competitions, spectacles, and military training. Begin was impressed by the splendor, and he proudly wore his brown Betar uniform. Betar was actively recruiting young people not only in Poland, but also in Romania, Czechoslovakia, Latvia, Brazil, Bulgaria, Germany, South Africa, Greece, Palestine, and the United States. By 1930, the organization had some 5,000 members in 21 countries; more than 40 percent of the members were students.[14] Despite these widely scattered cells, the most active areas of recruitment and other activities were in Palestine and Poland.

Begin became active in the Betar movement and soon rose to manage the Betar cell in Brisk. He first saw Jabotinsky when he was 16, during Jabotinsky's visit to Begin's hometown. Menachem was not the only member of the Begin household to be impressed by the dynamic Jabotinsky. Zeev-Dov also supported the Betar leader and his ideals, and he made a weekly donation (often collecting coins from friends and neighbors) for Jabotinsky's efforts.

LAW STUDENT

In 1931, Begin went to Warsaw, the capital of Poland. He was 18 years old and had enrolled as a law student at Warsaw University. Despite the demands of his studies, Begin remained active in Betar and soon landed a paid job at Betar's large Warsaw office. He proved himself an effective organizer and, perhaps more important, a gifted and polished orator. His speeches blended a stirring recitation of Jewish history and international politics with the ideals and aims of Betar.

In Warsaw, at Betar, Begin first served as head of the administration department. Occasionally, he skipped class to work in Betar's rather unimpressive offices. It was not the pay that motivated Begin—he made far less than the average salary for the type of work he was doing. Rather, he saw the opportunity to be a part of a movement that, he was convinced, would lead to the creation

Above, Israeli settlers celebrate the founding of a new Jewish kibbutz settlement in Yazur, Israel, in 1949. When Menachem Begin was a young man, in the 1930s, he considered moving to what was then British-controlled Palestine to join the Zionist movement. Settlements such as the one depicted above took place both before and after the official establishment of the state of Israel.

of a Jewish state. Each morning he arrived at the office with a slice of buttered bread and a hard-boiled egg, which he would eat while working.

By September 1935, Begin had been promoted to head of the propaganda department, a job well suited to his skills. In late 1937, the thirteenth anniversary of the founding of Betar, Begin graduated from the university. At this time, he helped organize a series of parades and demonstrations all around Poland. Begin spoke at many of the meetings, most significantly in the city of Lodz when the scheduled speaker did not arrive on time. The speech he made, delivered in Yiddish, Hebrew, and Polish, marked his rise as one of the leaders of the Betar organization. The audience was transfixed, and when he finished, they broke into thunderous applause.

At the time, Jewish forces were fighting with the British, who were attempting to maintain peace between Arab and Jewish settlers in Palestine. Betar organized a demonstration in Warsaw to show its support for the underground Jewish army operating similarly to a guerrilla force in Palestine. The demonstration culminated with a protest outside the British Embassy in Warsaw. Begin was at the head of the group marching to the embassy.

The Polish police arrived to break up the demonstration. Begin was arrested, interrogated, and then locked in a cell, where he remained for several weeks. Eventually, his release was arranged by numerous friends.

Begin quickly returned to work at Betar's propaganda department. There, he turned out material that connected events in Poland with those in Palestine, and he continued to drum up support for the Jewish guerilla force fighting the British in Palestine. Later, in 1937, he was sent to replace the leader of Betar in Czechoslovakia. He used his skills to recruit and organize the scattered Betar cell there before returning to Poland.

Many young men Begin's age had immigrated to Palestine. Indeed, the Zionist movement strongly urged Jews to come to Palestine to reclaim their ancestral homeland. Begin had a different plan for himself, however. He obtained his license to practice law in Poland. Despite his continued involvement with Betar, he was hired by a law firm. He seemed to be torn between a desire to build a life for himself in Poland and a passionate belief that Jews must join together to create a state for themselves in Palestine.

CHAPTER 4

Military Muscle

Anwar Sadat graduated from Egypt's Royal Military Academy in February 1938. As a new soldier, he was stationed in Manqabad, a small town in northern Egypt. When Sadat arrived in Manqabad, all the junior officers' rooms had already been assigned, so he was given a larger room, the kind normally assigned to more senior officers.

Sadat's room soon became a gathering place for many of the junior officers. They were all young men, most in their teens, and many were away from home for the first time. They were bored and restless. Sadat soon seized on that opportunity—an opportunity that his hero, Atatürk, had also utilized. Sadat used those gatherings in his room to spark the revolution he felt was needed in Egypt.

At first, the conversations focused on the occupation of Egypt by the British and how it directly affected those in the army. There were discussions of the injustice of the absolute power of the British military. There were complaints about the senior officers in the Egyptian army and their willingness to do whatever the British told them to do. It was this group that gathered in Sadat's room that would form

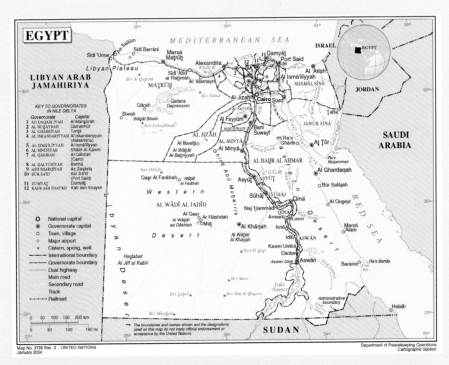

The map above shows Anwar Sadat's Egyptian homeland. As a young soldier, Sadat was stationed in Manqabad, a small town in northern Egypt.

the base of the Free Officers' Organization, which, 14 years later, would overthrow the government.

Among those gathered in Sadat's quarters was a serious young man named Gamal Abdel Nasser, who joined the meetings when his battalion was stationed in Manqabad. As the circle widened, Nasser continued to attend the meetings; he listened with interest, but said little.

In early 1939, Sadat was one of a few officers picked to attend a course in army signals conducted near Cairo. Nasser was also in the group. The Signals Corps was a new division within the army, and participation was considered an honor. After two and a half months of study, Sadat passed the exam and was chosen to join the Signals Corps.

Sadat seized this opportunity to expand his network of contacts. Being stationed near Cairo offered many advantages; for instance, he could hold meetings at his father's house, as well as at the Officers' Club, at cafes, and in the homes of other participants. The group, which became known as the Free Officers' Organization, attracted both junior and senior officers with the message that the Egyptian military should launch an armed revolution against the British occupation of Egypt.

As Sadat's group secretly began to discuss the idea of a revolt against British occupation, the British were facing a more visible threat—Hitler's Germany, which attacked Poland in September 1939. As Poland's allies, Britain and France declared war on Germany. When Italy entered the war as a German ally, the Egyptian army was sent to the western desert to prepare a line of defense against German and Italian forces.

Sadat was one of many Egyptians who saw the irony in this situation. To them, the occupying British were their true enemy, yet they were being forced to fight for the British against Germany and Italy. Sadat was sent to Marsa Matruh in northern Egypt, along the Mediterranean, to serve as a signals officer in an artillery brigade. His political activity continued and expanded there.

Many prominent Egyptians vocalized their anger over the war. The British sensed the danger and directed the Egyptian forces to pull back from the Mediterranean. The soldiers were ordered to hand over their weapons as they withdrew. The army viewed this as a humiliating request, and many who had not previously supported Sadat's plans for revolt now joined him. The Egyptian officers made it clear—they would not give up their weapons without a fight. The order was withdrawn.

A FAILED REVOLT

The British decision to back down on the weapons order inspired Sadat to begin to put his plan for revolution into effect. During the summer of 1941, as the Egyptian troops were withdrawing from Marsa Matruh, Sadat spread the word that the withdrawing troops should reassemble at a point near the highway leading into Cairo. They would then march into the capital city, force out the British, and take over the government.

At the appointed time, Sadat led his military unit from Marsa Matruh to Alexandria. They spent the night there, then traveled on to the designated gathering place outside Cairo. When Sadat and his unit arrived at the meeting place, however, no other units were present, nor did any arrive as he waited with his men. The glorious march on Cairo never took place. When no one else appeared, Sadat and his men were forced to disband and go home.

The failed attempt did not discourage Sadat. He continued his efforts, and the Free Officers' Organization continued to expand. An attempt to make contact with the Germans also did not materialize, and Sadat was arrested. The authorities had no definite evidence linking Sadat to the plot, however, and he was released.

It was not the last time that Sadat and his network would attempt to link up with the Germans. By 1942, German forces, under the command of Field Marshal Erwin Rommel, were in North Africa, and it was clear that the vast majority of Egyptians secretly hoped for a German invasion of Egypt. In February 1942, the British ordered King Farouk to ask the leader of the Egyptian parliament to form a new government—one that would be more cooperative. When the king refused, British tanks surrounded his palace, and he was ordered to cooperate or abdicate. The king reluctantly agreed to cooperate.

As anti-British sentiment grew, Rommel's army beat back the British and advanced as far as El Alamein, 65 miles from Alexandria. Egyptians took to the streets shouting, "Advance Rommel!" The British prepared to leave Egypt; they burned their official papers and departed for Sudan. Rumors began to spread that once Egypt fell, it would be given to Italy as part of the spoils of war. Although there was relief that the British might finally be leaving Egypt, Sadat and his supporters had no intention of allowing one occupying force to replace another.

Instead, they decided to attempt to negotiate with Rommel, to offer their military support for the German war effort in exchange for independence. Sadat, at the age of 22, helped draft a treaty. With it, he included aerial photographs showing British military positions. The treaty and photographs were then given to a pilot to transport to Rommel. To Sadat's misfortune, the Germans spotted the plane. Identifying it as a British-made aircraft, it was quickly shot down. The message never reached Rommel.

Sadat made one final attempt to communicate with Rommel. He was introduced to two Germans living in Egypt and learned that they possessed radio transmitters. Neither of the transmitters functioned, but Sadat thought that one of them might be repairable, so he took it home with him to better examine it and try to fix it.

What Sadat did not know was that British intelligence officers were tracking the two Germans. Shortly after meeting with them, he learned that they had been arrested. Sadat hid the transmitter in his study, but later that night, a group of Egyptian and British officers burst into his father's home. The officers searched the premises, and as they neared the study, Sadat explained that that room was occupied by female members of his family, and they would need to leave before the room could be searched. When the officers agreed, Sadat entered the study and quickly seized the transmitter and some gunpowder. He slipped them to his brother, who smuggled them out of the house.

Although the officers found nothing incriminating, Sadat was still arrested. After a court martial, he was dismissed from the Egyptian army, and thrown into prison. It was October 1942, and Sadat's struggle to achieve Egyptian independence seemed to have come to an end.

ANOTHER PERSPECTIVE

Menachem Begin had also been caught up in the war, but his experience began quite differently. In April 1939, he had become so powerful within the Betar organization that he was appointed head of Betar in Poland. He traveled from one Polish branch of Betar to another, encouraging supporters and trying to persuade undecided Jews of the righteousness of Betar's mission. To save money, he stayed in the homes of Betar members. It was as a guest in one of those homes that he met Aliza Arnold, the daughter of his host. One month after their meeting, on May 29, 1939, Aliza and Begin were married. Instead of wedding attire, the couple wore their brown Betar uniforms.

As a resident of Warsaw, Begin was well aware of the anti-Semitism that was increasingly and openly expressed. He encouraged Betar to set up an organization to streamline the emigration of Jews from Poland to Palestine, but the borders were closing, and on September 1, 1939, the German army invaded Poland.

Many Jews recognized the German invasion as a dangerous development. The Begins managed to obtain exit visas in early September. They packed a small sack with some clothes and a few essentials and went to the train station. They boarded the only available train, which was so packed that they were forced to crawl in through a window. It was dusk when they entered, but the train did not begin to move for several hours. Even after the train departed from the station, it stopped periodically as German planes attempted to bomb the tracks. Finally, Begin, Aliza, and the friends they were traveling with decided that they would be safer on foot.

They walked east and eventually reached a town, where they were warned by a Betar member who recognized them that the area was surrounded by Germans. It was night, but they decided to continue walking in the same direction and only stopped for short rests. They continued walking for several days, encountering streams of refugees heading south, while military convoys headed north.

By September 13, they had reached Vlodava, a town on the Polish border with Ukraine. They learned that Germans were already in Ukraine and decided to continue traveling east. Occasionally, a friendly farmer would give them a ride. Their goal was to try to reach Romania, from where they might be able to travel to Palestine.

Begin and his friends learned that Soviet troops were moving into the region through which they were traveling. At the time, they were uncertain which occupying force posed a greater danger to them—the Germans, who had vowed to force the Jews out of Europe (but might allow them to emigrate to Palestine), or the Soviets, who would not allow Jews to leave at all and would certainly view Begin's outspoken criticism of Communism with disfavor.

Begin's prominence as a Betar leader made him vulnerable to recognition, and he was soon denounced and arrested. He was released after a few days, and he and Aliza decided to travel to Vilna, in Lithuania, where they believed they would be safe. They arrived on October 28, 1939, and remained there for nearly a year, until Soviet forces annexed Lithuania, along with Latvia and Estonia. On September 1, 1940, one year after German troops invaded Poland, Begin was summoned to the town hall. He ignored the request, and soon afterward realized that his house was being watched and he was being followed.

Finally, the night came when officials knocked on his door. Begin was ordered to come with them. Despite their assurances that he would only need to come with them for a short time, Begin prepared for a longer absence. He put on his suit, polished his shoes, and gathered some food. He also took two books, the Bible and a biography written in English, which he was learning to read. He was 27 years old, and Aliza was only 20. He calmly said good-bye to his wife. Nearly two years would pass before he would see her again.

The Soviet officials who had seized Begin were well aware of his involvement with Betar. They questioned him at length, accused him of plotting activities against the Soviets in Vilna, and urged him to write a full confession. He was held for nearly three days without food, water, or sleep, then transported to the Lukishki Prison.

Above, Hitler visits the town of Danzig, Poland, in September 1939, shortly after his troops invaded Poland. When the Nazis invaded, Menachem Begin and his wife recognized the danger and were able to obtain exit visas in order to leave the country.

In his memoir, *White Nights,* Begin told the story of his imprisonment. Unlike many prisons, where those in captivity wondered *when* they would get out, Soviet prisoners wondered *whether* they would get out at all. Soviet captives were not concerned with what they would be questioned about; instead, they worried about what methods of torture would be used. Begin wrote:

> Regimes may come and go, but prison goes on for ever, although changes occur within its walls. When a revolution succeeds, the gates of the prisons are opened and the prisoners, victims of the regime that has just fallen, go free; literally on their heels, the gates close on new prisoners, victims of the regime that has just been set up. Humanity is still waiting for the revolution of revolutions that will not exchange prisoners but will do away with prisons.[15]

CHAPTER 5

Terrorists and Revolutionaries

As war swept over much of the world, both Menachem Begin and Anwar Sadat found themselves in prison. Sadat was located in British-occupied Egypt, and Begin in Soviet-occupied Lithuania. In Lukishki Prison, Begin rapidly lost weight due to the meager rations. He was questioned intensely about his involvement with Betar and forced to defend Zionism. He was deprived of sleep and moved from cell to cell. On April 1, 1941, Begin was informed in writing that he had been found to be "a dangerous element to society." He was sentenced to eight years in a work camp.

Aliza was able to smuggle packages to Menachem periodically. Most contained clothing—items like handkerchiefs and underwear. In one package, Begin discovered a handkerchief embroidered with the letters "OLA." He knew that this was some sort of message but puzzled over it for some time. He soon realized that the letters referred to the Hebrew word *olah,* meaning "going up." Jews referred to the journey to Palestine as "going up." Aliza was sending him a message that she was safe, and traveling to Palestine.

Begin and a large group of prisoners were transferred to a labor camp in the frozen north of the Soviet Union, where they worked 16-hour days. Their job was to unload iron train cars from boats in the river and then reload them onto flat cars. All of Begin's possessions, with the exception of the clothes he was wearing, were taken from him. He was ill frequently.

By that time, however, the Soviet Union was at war with Germany. One day, Begin and a group of other Polish citizens were released from the work camp. Begin embarked on the long march across the Soviet Union and back to Poland. He had no money, so he walked, pausing to sleep in parks or stairways. He found his sister in Russia. They soon learned that they were the only members of their family to survive the war. Begin would never learn exactly what happened to his mother, father, and brother.

Menachem Begin had only one option for legally leaving Russia, and he took it. He enlisted in the Free Polish Army, which was in Russia, gathering men to fight the Germans.

ESCAPE FROM PRISON

Anwar Sadat was sent to prison in 1942 and spent the next two years there. Gamal Abdel Nasser took over the Free Officers' Organization while Sadat was incarcerated.

Conditions in the first prison were not too bad. Sadat's cell contained a bed, blankets, and a small table and chair. He was allowed to smoke, although his cigarettes had to be lit by a prison guard because prisoners were not allowed to have matches in their possession. He was given newspapers and books to read, and could exercise twice a day for 15-minute periods. He decided to learn English, so he requested books in that language to help him improve his skills.

Gamal Abdel Nasser, pictured above shortly before his death in 1970, took over the Free Officers' Organization while Sadat was incarcerated in 1942. Nasser became the leader of Egypt in 1954 and remained in that position until his death.

Sadat was then moved to another prison in northern Egypt, about 160 miles from Cairo. He was held there from December 1942 to early November 1943. His family was only allowed to visit once a month. Sadat passed the time by teaching himself German as well as English. Late in 1943, Sadat and several prisoners were transferred to a different detention center, this time near Cairo. He and five other prisoners decided to organize an escape. They were recaptured after the first attempt, but they tried again and were successful.

From October 1944 to September 1945, Sadat lived as a fugitive. He grew a beard and took the name Hadji Muhammad. He worked a series of odd jobs, including loading and unloading trucks, building roads and a canal, and working at a quarry.

When World War II came to an end, martial law was lifted in Egypt, and Sadat was now a free man. He returned at last to his father's home and resumed his true identity. He also took up his plans to overthrow British rule once again. As a free man, Sadat wanted to resume control of the Free Officers' Organization, but he and Nasser soon clashed over the direction of the organization. Sadat believed that only through violence—through terrorist activities—would Egypt be able to achieve independence. Nasser disagreed. Sadat proposed that the Free Officers plant a bomb in the British Embassy when the ambassador was in residence. Nasser refused.

Next, Sadat targeted several prominent, pro-British politicians for assassination, including Egyptian premier Mustafa Nahas Pasha. A grenade was thrown under the premier's car, but did not explode on time, and the premier escaped unharmed. In 1946, Sadat targeted the Egyptian finance minister, Amin Osman, who was shot and killed. Sadat's part in the plot was quickly uncovered, and he was arrested and jailed, this time in Cell 54 of Cairo's infamous Central Prison.

The conditions in Central Prison were far different from those Sadat had experienced in previous detention centers. Before, he had been jailed as a political prisoner; this time, he was guilty of participating in the murder of a prominent Egyptian politician. There was no bed in Cell 54, only a thin mat and a dirty blanket on the floor. That was the only furniture in the room. The prison was infested with bugs, and water seeped out from the walls. Sadat was given no newspapers and no radio. His only contact with other humans occurred once a day, during a 15-minute walk on the prison grounds during which the prisoners were allowed to talk to each other. Sadat spent 18 months in the prison, unable to read or write and incapable of receiving any news of the outside world.

"Two places in this world make it impossible for a man to escape from himself," Sadat wrote in his memoirs, "a battlefield and a prison cell."[16] Sadat took advantage of the isolation and his loneliness to focus on his life, to evaluate where he was and what he wanted to accomplish. He evaluated his marriage and realized it had been a mistake. When conditions improved in the prison, and Sadat was allowed visitors and some reading materials, he asked his wife not to visit. Later, when he was released from prison, the couple divorced.

With the return of reading materials, Sadat avidly devoured books, newspapers, and magazines. He focused on reading in English in an effort to improve his skills. He also taught himself French. Sadat would later look back on this time of introspection, of study and evaluation, as a great period in his personal growth. He would describe his last eight months in prison as "the happiest period in my life."[17]

A NEW STATE

While Sadat was in prison, a new state had been created in the territory known as Palestine. That state was known as Israel. Its creation was the culmination of a dream for Menachem Begin. He had joined the Free Polish Army and was quickly transported to fight in the Middle East. Begin's unit traveled through Iran and Iraq, arriving in Palestine in May 1942. There, he was joyfully reunited with his wife. On March 1, 1943, Aliza gave birth to the couple's first child, a son they named Benjamin.

Begin reestablished contact with colleagues from his days with Betar, many of whom began to press him to leave the Polish army and join the struggle to gain the release of Palestine from British control. His release from the army was arranged through a friend, and he quickly joined the IZL, the underground army dedicated to forcing the British out of Palestine. IZL was the abbreviation for *Irgun Zvai Leumi,* Hebrew for "National Military Organization."

In December 1943, at the age of 30, Begin was named head of the IZL. The rise of anti-Semitism in Europe and the systematic effort by Nazi Germany to exterminate its Jewish population would become the subtext of the struggle for Begin and many other Jews in Palestine. Begin wrote in his memoir of those years, titled *The Revolt*:

> When we launched our revolt against the yoke of oppression and against the wanton shedding of Jewish blood we were convinced that our people truly had nothing to lose except the prospect of extermination. . . . This was not a mere phrase of hyperbole. It was the truth; and it strengthened immeasurably the rebels' capacity for sacrifice. Capacity for sacrifice is the measure of revolt and the father of victory . . . in all history there is no greater force than the readiness for self-sacrifice, just as there is no greater love than the love of freedom. The soil of their country and the blood of their murdered people infused the Hebrew rebels with both that force and that love.[18]

Begin quickly began to adopt new strategies for the IZL. He aimed to create a more cohesive, secret organization. He believed that Germany would soon be defeated, and he wanted to be ready for the war he knew would follow: the war to create a Jewish state in Palestine.

THE CONFLICT BEGINS

During World War II, the British government developed a policy for Palestine in which a balance of numbers had to be preserved between the Arab and Jewish populations. This meant that many Jews who managed to escape Nazi-occupied regions of Europe were turned away at the border.

The policy infuriated the Jews living in Palestine. They knew there were almost no other safe havens available to Jewish refugees. It was this policy that in large part inspired plans for armed revolt against the British in Palestine.

Begin was living in Jerusalem at the time. The IZL was based in Tel Aviv, so Begin spent weekdays living in a hotel near the Tel Aviv waterfront. On weekends, he returned home to his family in Jerusalem. Neighbors believed that he was working in a law office in Tel Aviv, but Begin's "work" would come to be defined by the British as terrorism.[19] Begin would dispute this definition, arguing that "terrorism" could not accurately be applied to what he called "a revolutionary war of liberation." He later wrote, "a revolution, or a revolutionary war, does not aim at instilling fear. Its object is to overthrow a regime and to set up a new regime in its place."[20]

Begin quickly reorganized the IZL into a more efficient paramilitary operation. Different units were assigned to different parts of the country, and a senior officer was given responsibility for each unit. Members were divided into propaganda warfare teams, assault teams, and recruitment and procurement teams.

Begin's philosophy was that, as long as Britain was at war with Germany, British military installations in Palestine should not be attacked. Because the ultimate goal was to ensure that Britain did not continue to occupy Palestine after the war had ended, however, the symbols of British authority in the country, such as government offices and police stations, were primary targets. A traitor informed on Begin, and his home in Jerusalem fell under British surveillance. The IZL was able to smuggle Aliza and the baby out, and they joined Begin in Tel Aviv.

On February 1, 1944, Begin published the IZL's formal declaration of war, which appeared on posters throughout Palestine. It called on Jewish youth to join their cause, urged Jews to call a general strike, for students to strike at the school, and for all Jews to refuse to pay any taxes to the British. It was, in short, a call for civil war. The British initially dismissed the threat, but they were soon forced to take it seriously. On February 12, explosions occurred almost simultaneously in Jerusalem, Haifa, and Tel Aviv. In all three cases, the targets were the immigration offices maintained by the British.

Begin then targeted the Palestine Police Criminal Investigation Department (CID), the heavily guarded local police stations that were well known for their brutality toward captured Jewish prisoners. In late March 1944, the CID offices in Tel Aviv, Haifa, and Jerusalem were all rocked by explosions. Not all members of the Jewish community in Palestine supported the guerilla tactics of this underground army. Many still believed that if they cooperated and negotiated with the British, they would be given the land to form a Jewish state once World War II had ended.

Begin continually selected symbolic dates and targets for the IZL's attacks. The British set a high reward for his capture, but he managed to avoid them. The family moved several times. Begin grew a beard and took on several different assumed names. While the family was living in hiding, Begin's second child, a daughter, was born. She was named Hasia, after Begin's mother. Begin could not register his daughter, because he could not provide her last name without revealing himself. He was also prohibited from going to the hospital for his daughter's birth. A friend carried the news of the baby's birth back to Begin, at first incorrectly informing him that he had a son.

As the war drew to a close, the different factions among the Jews in Palestine became increasingly antagonistic. Each was convinced that their approach was the only way to bring about the creation of a Jewish homeland in Palestine. The IZL was soon under surveillance not only by the British, but also by

Menachem Begin led many of the IZL's efforts in their revolt against the British, including an attack that targeted the King David Hotel, where the British maintained the headquarters of their Palestinian operations. About 100 people were killed in the explosion; another 100 were wounded.

other Jewish groups that were determined to bring their violent actions to an end. The result was a kind of civil war, pitting those sympathetic to the IZL against those who believed that cooperation with the British would be more effective. Many IZL members were seized and turned over to the British, but Begin refused to retaliate.

Begin also began to reach out to the Arab population of Palestine. He wanted to defuse the British government's potential argument that they needed to remain in Palestine to keep the peace between its Jewish and Arab populations. In posters placed around Palestine, the IZL stressed that its war was with the British occupiers and no one else.

Finally, the leaders of the various factions within the Jewish community in Palestine decided to cooperate. Their combined effort at revolt lasted from November 1945 until September 1946. Although the IZL acted independently, Begin met biweekly with the leaders of the two other Jewish groups to plan strategy and determine the targets for their attacks. World War II had ended, so British military installations were now deemed acceptable targets.

Begin also targeted the King David Hotel in Jerusalem, a six-story luxury hotel where the British maintained the headquarters of their Palestinian operations. About 100 people were killed in the explosion and another 100 wounded. The attack at the King David Hotel prompted public condemnation of the IZL. British soldiers were ordered to boycott Jewish-owned businesses and restaurants. The boycott, and the anti-Semitism displayed by many British officers in enforcing it, triggered a backlash and united the various Jewish groups against the British. This feeling intensified in August 1946, when British armed divisions moved into Tel Aviv to stage a manhunt for three leading figures of the Jewish revolt. One of them was Menachem Begin.

Armed troops and police set up barbed wire, splitting the city into sectors. They went from house to house, searching for Begin. A curfew was enacted, and many Jews were arrested. Begin hid in a secret panel installed in the ceiling of his bathroom for nearly three days while British soldiers searched his home.

Begin escaped, and the IZL campaign against the British intensified. In mid-1947, the United Nations (UN) sent a delegation to Palestine to help determine how the unrest in that country could best be resolved. Several of the delegates met with Begin, and he was given the opportunity to explain to these international diplomats the aims of the IZL and the organization's views on why Palestine should become a Jewish state.

and one Jewish. The newly created Arab state, centered largely on the West Bank of the Jordan River, would become part of what was then called "Transjordan." (Today, it is the country known as Jordan.) The Jewish state would become the state of Israel.

The borders of the partitioned Palestine were especially contentious. Slightly more than 55 percent of what had once been Palestine was apportioned to the Jewish state, even though Jews made up less than 30 percent of the population. A small stretch of land on the Mediterranean Sea, known as the Gaza Strip, would be granted to Egypt. The city of Jerusalem, holy to both Jews and Arabs, would belong to neither state, but instead would be "internationalized."

As war broke out, Anwar Sadat followed the developments from his prison cell. His trial was under way. It lasted eight months, from January to August 1948. He was finally acquitted of all charges after 31 months in jail. After his release, he spent some time readjusting to normal life. At first, he moved to the town of Hilwan, where he spent a period away from friends and family in order to take time to gradually make decisions about his life.

Finally, a friend named Hassan Izzat found Sadat in Hilwan and urged him to return with him to his home in Suez. It was there that Sadat met Hassan's cousin, a young woman named Jehan Raouf. She was 15 when they met, and he was 15 years her senior. She wrote in her memoirs of her meeting with the man she had heard so much about, stating:

> I knew I should drop my eyes, not look at this man—or any man, for that matter—in a bold manner, but at the moment I had no control. It was dark in the hall, but his features were so familiar to me from all the photographs I had seen that it seemed as if the lights were blazing. His eyes resting on mine looked solemn and sad, and I could not look away. His face, even darker in hue than it had appeared in his photographs, seemed burdened with the world.[22]

On May 29, 1949, Jehan Raouf and Anwar Sadat married.

On February 24, 1949, an armistice was signed that brought an end to the Arab–Israeli war. Israel had fought fiercely against the invading Arab forces and eventually pushed the armies back, its army occupying additional stretches of Arab land. As part of the terms of that armistice, Israel was given the right to continue to occupy land it had seized during the war—an additional 2,000 square miles (5,180 square kilometers). Other land was divided among the Arab nations: 140 square miles (363 square kilometers) in the Gaza Strip was given to Egypt; 2,270 square miles (5,879 square kilometers) of what had once been East Jerusalem and eastern Palestine (later known as the West Bank), were granted to Jordan.

Borders now marked much of the region. The city of Jerusalem was divided between Jordanian and Israeli territory. Demilitarized zones were set up in Jerusalem, as well as along the borders between Israel and Syria and between Israel and Egypt. In 1950, tensions were further inflamed when Israel moved its capital from Tel Aviv to Jerusalem.

The defeat in the war had proved particularly humiliating for the Egyptian military, which had formed a significant portion of the invading force. The Egyptian people had expected that victory over Israel would be quick and decisive. They had not been prepared for a long war, nor had they anticipated that it would lead to defeat and the loss of a portion of their land. In addition, Egypt was facing a budget deficit.

Egypt's King Farouk was not able to adequately respond to the challenges of a defeated, demoralized army and an angry populace. His government was already facing charges of corruption. He attempted to turn the anger of his people away from himself and toward a convenient target: the British.

RETURN TO MILITARY LIFE

The Free Officers remained active while Sadat was in prison. Gamal Nasser became the organization's leader, and the group continued to plot to gain independence. Sadat soon resumed his involvement with the Free Officers. In 1950, his military commission was restored, and in 1952, he was promoted to lieutenant colonel. Both the army and the Free Officers wanted to use Sadat to report on the activities of the other, and he served as a double agent, providing Nasser and the Free Officers with information about the army while pretending to serve as a spy.

Anger at the British presence in Egypt continued to build. King Farouk assisted in fanning these flames in subtle ways. Anti-British rallies and riots were held along the Suez Canal, where the British military had its bases, and British troops patrolling the canal were subject to attacks.

On January 25, 1952, Britain ordered all armed Egyptians, including Egyptian police, out of the town of Ismailia. King Farouk ordered the police to resist the order, and 50 Egyptian policemen were killed in the ensuing violence.

Riots erupted in Cairo, and the violence soon spread throughout Egypt. Such unrest presented an opportunity, one Nasser and the Free Officers determined to seize. Sadat was on military duty in the Gaza area when he received a message from Nasser, summoning him to Cairo. He arrived on July 22, 1952, eventually making contact with Nasser and helping to coordinate the various units of the Free Officers as they enacted their quick and bloodless takeover of the government.

On the morning of July 23, 1952, Sadat's voice announced over the radio that the Free Officers of Cairo were now in control of the government of Egypt, and he demanded the king's resignation. In his memoirs, Sadat wrote of this moment:

> The dream on which I had lived for years—a dream to which I devoted my entire life—had finally materialized. It was now a reality surging in my heart, possessing my being and dwarfing it. Everything else paled, was pushed into the shadows, while that reality alone shone bright, rising high and majestic and towering above all else.[23]

Sadat is pictured in coat and tie at back, seated, in this photograph of some of the leaders who led the revolt in Egypt in 1952. Nasser is also seated at the table, third from the right.

Despite Sadat's role in announcing the revolution, it was Nasser who was firmly in control of Egypt in the years that followed independence. Egypt's first president was a popular military man, Major-General Muhammad Naguib, but Nasser was in control behind the scenes. In 1954, he took over the government.

During those years, Sadat helped in a number of minor posts, but he was never given a prominent position in Nasser's government. Sadat edited the government newspaper, *Al Gomhouria*, writing a number of anti-American editorials. He served as secretary general of the Islamic Congress, as well as minister of the state from 1954 to 1956. In 1957, he was named secretary general of the National Union. Because his dreams of revolution had been realized, Sadat was no longer at the center of things. He had become a kind of figurehead, a symbol of a revolution that was over.

PARTY SHAPER

The state of Israel had been established and the Arab forces defeated. It seemed clear that Menachem Begin needed to find a new role for himself and for those he had led for many years. A victorious Israeli army did not need a second, underground army operating within its borders. Independence had been achieved. Israelis now needed to come together to build the new nation.

Begin knew that he needed to find a new role. He did not have a license to practice law in Israel, nor did he have an inclination to return to the profession he had studied so many years before. At the same time, he still had strong ideas about how Israel should be governed, ideas that in many cases differed from those of the government in power, led by David Ben-Gurion.

In time, Begin decided to form a new political party. It would be called *Herut,* meaning "Freedom." Begin announced its formation on June 2, 1948, and quickly set to work transforming his underground fighters into political activists capable of working with Israel's parliamentary political system.

Begin emerged from hiding and soon embarked on a speaking tour. He traveled across Israel to share the message of Herut. The new political leaders of Israel were outraged at this challenge to their accomplishments. Israel's first elections for its Parliament, known as the Knesset, were held in 1949. Herut won 13 percent of the national vote, and Begin joined the Knesset.

Herut's platform focused on the ideal of an unpartitioned Israel. Its party insignia showed an outline of the completed Israel occupying both sides of the Jordan River. Herut favored the idea of war until all of this "Land of Israel" was reunited. Over the years, this concept would fade, and the focus would be on claiming the West Bank and Gaza.

Herut Party economic policies favored national health insurance, a right to work, equal rights for minorities, and freedom of religion and culture. Begin did not believe in the separation of religion and state, however, and his party could not be described as secular.

In those early years after independence, Israel's economy was foundering. Huge numbers of Jews had immigrated to Israel. Natural resources were in short supply, and industry was not yet developed. The war with the Arab nations had further stretched the young nation's finances.

Finally, in 1952, a proposal was made by some within the Israeli government: Israel should ask Germany to make reparations for Jewish property and lives lost when the Nazis were in power. Begin and the Herut Party were determined to defeat this plan, believing that Israel should not give Germany the opportunity to rehabilitate itself in the world's eyes by making this gesture, nor should Israel's economy be dependent on a handout from the nation that had destroyed the families of so many Israelis. Many Israelis who had not previously been supporters of Begin's party joined him in protesting the decision.

Begin led a rally outside the Knesset before stepping inside to join the debate. He expressed to the crowd that, "A Jewish government that negotiates with Germany can no longer be a Jewish government."[24] As the crowd threw stones at the Knesset building and riots broke out, Begin argued inside with David Ben-Gurion, the prime minister, calling him a "hooligan."[25] He eventually retracted the remark, but urged the prime minister to hold a referendum rather than taking an action that, he believed, was against the will of most Israelis. Begin argued that "from a Jewish point of view there is not a single German who is not a Nazi, and there is not a single German who is not a murderer. And you are going to them to receive money."[26]

Begin's efforts were unsuccessful. The Knesset voted to negotiate with Germany to receive payments as restitution. Begin continued to protest the decision and was ultimately suspended

Pictured above is David Ben-Gurion, the first prime minister of Israel. Begin called Ben-Gurion a "hooligan" during debates in the Knesset, in which Begin protested Ben-Gurion's willingness to negotiate with the government of Germany.

from taking part in Knesset activities for two weeks. His critics labeled him as an "extremist," someone who did not respect the parliamentary procedures of the Knesset. Ben-Gurion refused to work with him. In parliamentary discussions or debates, the prime minister refused even to speak Begin's name. If he needed to refer to Begin, he used phrases like "the man sitting next to Dr. Bader" (another Herut member).[27]

Herut would remain an opposition party until 1977. Begin was comfortable in the minority and with the act of challenging the status quo. He was outspoken in his opinions of government decisions, one of which was over the proper response to events in Egypt. In 1955, Nasser had signed an arms deal with Czechoslovakia. The deal enabled Egypt to import Soviet arms and weapons via Czechoslovakia. Nasser made no attempt to dispute the evidence that these weapons would eventually be used against Israel.

Begin made it clear that he thought Israel should strike immediately and not wait for Egypt to make its intentions clear. He announced at one rally in Tel Aviv, "War is preferable now rather than waiting for the day when the Arabs attack us."[28]

Gradually, Ben-Gurion began to agree. The Israeli prime minister formed a plan to cross into Egypt and attack the Egyptian military based in the Sinai Desert. The hope was that British and French troops would ultimately intervene in the crisis and take over the Suez Canal, which Nasser had recently seized and nationalized. Shortly before the invasion took place, Ben-Gurion made the unprecedented gesture of inviting Begin to his home, where he revealed the details of his plan, then asked for his support. Begin agreed.

On October 29, 1956, Israel launched its attack on Egypt and invaded Sinai. The United Nations Security Council passed a resolution calling on Israel to withdraw from Egypt, but the resolution was vetoed by France and Britain. The Sinai–Suez War was under way.

By November 5, Israel had seized control of the Gaza Strip and other strategic points along the Sinai Peninsula. French and British troops occupied the Canal Zone, which separated Egypt from the Sinai. Nasser was forced to accept a humiliating cease-fire.

CHAPTER 7

Rise to
Power

hereas Begin spent several decades openly criticizing his nation's leadership when he disagreed with policy decisions, Sadat served patiently and quietly in whatever role he was given. He was loyal to Nasser and never aired any private disagreements he may have had with Egypt's leader. "Never in my whole career did I prefer one post to another on account of 'power,'" he wrote in his memoirs. "I would serve in any capacity as long as I knew it was for the good of Egypt—Speaker, Deputy Speaker, or member were all the same to me. What counted was what I did, not the post I held."[29]

Egypt was firmly allied with the Soviet Union. In 1966, however, the United States extended an invitation to Sadat, who was serving as Egypt's Speaker of the National Assembly at the time, to visit the country. It seemed an opportunity to ease tensions between the United States and Egypt, and Sadat, with Nasser's approval, accepted.

War with Israel broke out again on June 5, 1967. It began, in part, as a conflict over access to water. A project in northern Israel to provide needed irrigation from the Sea of Galilee sparked protest from Syria, as some of the work was taking place in the demilitarized zone separating the two nations. At almost the same time, to the east of

Israel, Jordan was constructing a large dam on the Yarmuk River, which empties into the Jordan River. (The Jordan River separates Israel and Jordan.) Israel protested the project, arguing that it would decrease the amount of water in the Jordan River.

Projects in Lebanon and Syria, such as one to divert the water flowing into the Jordan River for other construction work, were attacked by Israel. It was a short step from water to weapons. Syrian troops began shelling Israeli settlers in the north, and Israel responded by launching an air attack and shooting down Syrian fighter planes.

At the time, Gamal Nasser was the most prominent figure in the Arab world, a spokesman for all issues involving Arab interests. He responded to the crisis by moving Egyptian troops into the Sinai Peninsula along the Israeli border and ordering the United Nations force that had been patrolling the border to leave.

On June 5, 1967, Israeli forces launched attacks against Syria, Jordan, Iraq, and Egypt. The attacks against the Egyptian air force were particularly ferocious, essentially eliminating them with a few overwhelming raids. Within three days, Egyptian forces were in retreat. Israel had seized Gaza and the Sinai territory, which lead almost all the way to the Suez Canal. Israeli forces seized all Jordanian territory west of the River Jordan, including the section of Jerusalem designated as Jordanian territory.

It was a bitter and humiliating defeat for the Egyptians, particularly for Nasser. Sadat described the period following this defeat, from June 1967 to September 1970, as one of

> intense suffering, unprecedented, I believe, in the entire stretch of Egyptian history. The suffering was engendered by a sense of frustration on the national, political, and military levels—so much so that a struggle for survival was the period's most distinctive feature. It is a man's sense of frustration that makes him, more than anything else, fight for survival.[30]

Nasser's health suffered after the defeat. Diabetes and severe pain in his legs made it difficult for him to function. In September 1969, he suffered a heart attack and doctors told him that he needed complete rest. Finally forced to confront his own mortality, Nasser turned to the loyal Sadat and appointed him vice president in December of that year.

Nasser attempted to confront the problems in the Egyptian military that had contributed to the defeat in the war with Israel. He discharged incompetent officers and replaced illiterate soldiers with more highly educated high school and university graduates. The pay offered to soldiers was increased, and discipline was more strictly enforced. Soviet advisers were also brought in to offer assistance. Each Egyptian military unit had a team of Soviet advisers assigned to it. The advisers included pilots, missile technicians, and engineers.

Dependence on the Soviets proved to be a double-edged sword for Nasser. The Soviets offered to supply weapons and aircraft, but they set the timetable for when those supplies would be delivered. The alliance with the Soviets had also forced Nasser to distance himself from the United States and Western Europe, which left Nasser with few options, should the Soviets prove unwilling to help him.

In September 1970, an Arab Summit was held in Cairo, and Nasser presided over it. The leaders of all Arab countries attended. Each ruler had a difficult personality, and Nasser felt a personal responsibility for drawing them all together. Libya's leader, Muammar Qaddafi, and Palestinian leader Yasir Arafat continually challenged the unity of the conference with their outbursts and conduct. As the summit drew to a close, Nasser was exhausted, yet he felt responsible for accompanying each leader to the airport.

Only hours after the conference ended, Nasser died of a heart attack. When summoned to Nasser's bedside and told of the leader's death, Sadat burst into tears. Sadat was then forced to make the funeral arrangements. A public outpouring of grief followed the announcement of Nasser's death. He had led Egypt for nearly 20 years and inspired revolutions in several other Arab nations. Mourning spread throughout the Arab world.

Above, crowds mass along the streets during the funeral for Egypt's beloved leader, Gamal Abdel Nasser. Nasser died suddenly of a heart attack on September 28, 1970.

Nine days after Nasser's death, Egypt's National Assembly formally voted to elect Anwar Sadat as the nation's leader. Nasser had dictated that presidential elections should only be held when, "the consequences of Israeli aggression had been removed."[31] Sadat initially supported this plan, stating that he would carry on as vice-president, but it soon became clear that rivals were plotting to seize power, and the country's leadership was still in question. A popular election was held, and on October 15, 1970, Sadat was elected president of Egypt.

CONFRONTING CRISIS

In Israel, the 1960s was a period when Begin settled into his role in the Knesset as the leader of the opposition. He was noted for always attending Knesset sessions, and his verbal skills served him well in parliamentary debates. He was courteous to his opponents, ate in the Knesset cafeteria, and still kept the same modest Tel Aviv apartment he had lived in for decades.

When Egypt threatened war in 1967, Begin and the Herut Party agreed to support the new prime minister, Levi Eshkol. On June 2, Begin was invited to join the emergency government cabinet as it prepared for the Six-Day War that would follow. He served as a minister without portfolio. As a minister without portfolio, Begin did not head a particular department. He had a small office on the floor above the prime minister. His position entitled him only to one secretary, a driver, and an office manager. He would remain in that position until July 1970.

When the war ended, Begin's dream of an Israel that stretched as far as the Jordan River, and a reunified Jerusalem, had become reality. He no longer seemed an extremist when he spoke of the "land of Israel." As a member of the National Unity government, Begin formed alliances with Defense Minister Moshe Dayan and, when Eshkol died a few months after the war ended, he was able to build a relationship with the newly elected prime minister, Golda Meir.

Begin's focus during this time was to ensure that Israel did not withdraw from the occupied territories. He viewed himself as a kind of watchdog, defending the Israel that had been created in the aftermath of the 1967 war.[32]

It was U.S. efforts to help negotiate a settlement in the Middle East that prompted Begin once more to assume an outspoken, critical role. On December 9, 1969, the United States announced its plan to settle the conflict between Israel and Egypt that had been simmering since the 1967 war, and at the same time attempt to step back from an elevation of tensions between the United States and the Soviet Union. U.S. president Richard Nixon had instructed his secretary of state, William Rogers, to attempt to determine whether the Soviets would be willing to help bring an end to the conflict in the region.

Rogers's proposal, known as "the Rogers Plan," called for the return of all occupied territories seized in 1967. It called for Israel to pull out of its occupation of east Jerusalem and restore Jerusalem as an "international" city. Begin responded with fiery rhetoric. He had long been a visible opponent to any idea of withdrawal from occupied territories and was openly critical of American and Soviet efforts to interfere with events in the Middle East.

In August 1970, Israel accepted a cease-fire along the Suez Canal, in addition to a partial Israeli withdrawal from the area. The day after the signing of the cease-fire, Begin resigned his ministerial post. Begin asked, "What happened to the government of Israel? What happened to the Jewish state?" and "Has this turned once again into a game in the hands of foreigners?"[33]

Ironically, Begin was not alone in his opposition to the Rogers Plan. Across the border, in Egypt, Anwar Sadat was equally opposed to any attempts by the United States and the Soviet Union to interfere with the politics of the Middle East.

CONFRONTING CHALLENGES

Nasser had been so successful at consolidating power and shaping the Egyptian presidency in his image that few could imagine an Egypt without Nasser at its head. Few expected that Sadat would be able to hold on to power, particularly when he was confronted with numerous rivals who believed they should be Egypt's next president.

Sadat began by putting an end to some of the particularly unpopular policies Nasser had used to maintain control. He ended the practice of seizure of property by the government and restored land to many from whom it had been taken. He put tighter controls on Egypt's notorious secret police and made it clear that criticism of the government would be tolerated rather than harshly punished.

Sadat gave many televised speeches to the nation, in which he projected an image of calm confidence. He appeared in public with his wife, with their three daughters and one son, and with their dogs, presenting himself as a more accessible leader.

Remembering how he himself had plotted the overthrow of an unpopular government, Sadat was careful to obtain the support of Egypt's military. He visited army installations, met with officers, and listened to their complaints.[34]

Sadat's policies made him very popular with the people, but the administration Sadat had inherited from Nasser was allied against him. Sadat's wife soon learned from friends that members of the government were plotting against her husband. The trouble increased when, four months after Sadat assumed the presidency, he announced a peace initiative. If Israel withdrew forces from the Sinai, Egypt would reopen the Suez Canal. Sadat also proposed to restore diplomatic relations with the United States.

One night, in fear and exasperation, Mrs. Sadat confronted her husband, and told him, "You are in a race with your enemies, and the winner will be the one who is quickest to get rid of the other." She went on to say, "You have forgotten something very important," to which Sadat replied, "God is with me."[35]

Sadat was soon able to purge the government of those plotting against him, but he could not so easily rid himself of the problems that had been Nasser's legacy. The economy was a disaster; the country's resources were so taxed that the government faced being unable to pay the salaries of civil employees and those serving in the military. Foreign policy was equally problematic; apart from other Arab nations, Egypt's only ally was the Soviet Union, and the Soviets were displeased with many of the policies Sadat had initiated.

Sadat met with Nikolai Podgorny, the president of the Soviet Union, in May 1971, and noted that the relationship with the Soviets needed to improve. He expressed his displeasure with the quality and quantity of weapons the Soviets had been supplying to the Egyptians. Podgorny told Sadat that he would be able to supply better weapons in four days' time. Sadat waited for nearly five months for the promised weapons, but they never arrived. His letters to Podgnory were not answered.

Leonid Brezhnev, the head of the Soviet government, met with U.S. President Richard Nixon in 1972. After the meeting, both leaders publicly called for a relaxation of tensions in the Middle East. Egypt, which had been receiving a great deal of military aid from the Soviet Union, promptly expelled the Soviet "military experts" and refused to accept any further assistance.

Sadat was invited to Moscow that October. Determined to resolve the situation one way or another, Sadat accepted the invitation and met again with the Soviet leadership, who promised him missile-equipped aircraft and experts to train Egyptians in their use. The year ended and 1972 began, and still there was no equipment from the Soviets.

As Sadat was waiting for weapons from the Soviets, Secretary of State William Rogers announced that the United States would supply Israel with weapons and military equipment, noting that the two countries would jointly manufacture arms in Israel.

Sadat returned to Moscow in February 1972, giving the Soviets one last chance. He would be disappointed. When the weapons finally arrived in May, they were not the ones that had been requested. Sadat was furious. Leonid Brezhnev, the head of the Soviet government, was meeting with U.S. President Nixon, and both leaders publicly called for a relaxation of tensions in the Middle East. Sadat interpreted this as a message that the Soviets would ship no additional weapons to Egypt, leaving Israel in a position of military superiority.

Sadat summoned the Soviet ambassador and told him that the 15,000 Soviet "military experts" currently in Egypt needed to leave. All Soviet-owned equipment currently in Egypt either needed to immediately be sold to Egypt or taken out of the country. All of this was to happen within one week.

In his memoirs, Sadat explained,

> The Soviets had thought at one time that they had Egypt in its pocket, and the world had come to think that the Soviet Union was our guardian. I wanted to tell the Russians that the will of Egypt was entirely Egyptian; I wanted to tell the whole world that we are always our own masters.[36]

ROAD TO WAR

Many interpreted Sadat's decision to expel the Soviet military advisers as an indication that Egypt would not attack Israel in the immediate future. They were wrong.

From the beginning of his presidency, Sadat had frequently threatened war with Israel. Secretary of State Rogers's announcement of military support for Israel was made partly in response to the belligerent speeches of Sadat. Nonetheless, when the war finally began, few were prepared for it.

As described at the beginning of this book, the October War of 1973 (also known as the Yom Kippur War) began on October 6, 1973, when Egyptian planes crossed the Canal. Although he had expelled the Soviet advisers in a show of strength, Sadat had not completely broken diplomatic relations with the Soviets, and the Soviet-supplied SAM-6 surface-to-air missiles would wreak heavy damage on Israeli aircraft.

Sadat supervised military operations from an office at the army headquarters, just outside Cairo. By the end of the first week, more than 1,000 Egyptian tanks and 100,000 soldiers occupied the east bank of the Suez Canal.

The initial success of Egyptian forces made Sadat tremendously popular in his country and throughout the Arab world. This time, Egyptian forces were confronting the powerful Israeli

Henry Kissinger

Menachem Begin and Anwar Sadat received the Nobel Prize for their efforts to carve out a peaceful solution to the conflict in the Middle East. President Jimmy Carter is recognized for his role in bringing the two men together at Camp David. But it was Henry Kissinger who first set the stage for peace through a series of individual meetings he held with various leaders in the Middle East following the 1967 war. Flying from one capital to another, Kissinger perfected what came to be known as "shuttle diplomacy," using his personal prestige to begin the process of defining the disputes that needed to be resolved in order for peace to be achieved.

Kissinger was born in Furth, Germany, in 1923. As a Jew, he was forced to flee Germany with his family when the Nazis came to power. He later joked that Anwar Sadat, who had learned German in prison, spoke with a better accent than he did. Kissinger was drafted into the army and became a U.S. citizen in 1943. He served with distinction in World War II, then returned to the United States and earned undergraduate and graduate degrees from Harvard.

Kissinger taught at Harvard, specializing in international relations, and he also worked for the Council of Foreign Relations. Kissinger became involved in politics through a friendship

army and winning. When Israel began to win back some territory, and the United States hurried to supply Israel, the Arab nations rallied around Egypt and introduced a new weapon into the Middle East conflict. This weapon was oil. Saudi Arabia and other petroleum-exporting nations agreed to cut back on shipments of oil to the United States.

A cease-fire was agreed to on October 22, but Sadat quickly charged Israel with violating the terms of the cease-fire. The new American secretary of state, Henry Kissinger, soon traveled to the region to meet with Sadat. The two men subsequently met numerous times and formed a relationship that would ultimately

with Nelson Rockefeller, serving on his campaign and also as an adviser on Vietnam during the Kennedy administration. President Richard Nixon appointed him to serve as his assistant for national security affairs, a position he held from 1969 to 1975. During much of the same time, Kissinger also served as secretary of state, holding that office from 1973 to 1977 under both Presidents Nixon and Gerald Ford.

Kissinger was awarded the Nobel Peace Prize in 1973. He shared it with Vietnamese negotiator Le Duc Tho; they were chosen for their efforts to bring an end to the war in Vietnam. The award would prove controversial—the two negotiators failed to bring about a lasting peace, and both men were viewed by many as having contributed as much to escalating the conflict as they ever did to bringing it to an end.

In recent years, Kissinger was invited to serve on the September 11 Commission, the nonpartisan commission formed in the aftermath of the terrorist attacks in New York and Washington on September 11, 2001. The panel was to investigate the events that contributed to the failure of the intelligence community in preventing these devastating events. Kissinger was forced to step down shortly after the appointment, however, when charges of a conflict of interest, connected to clients of his consulting business, called into question his ability to provide unbiased leadership to the committee.

pave the way for new communications between Egypt and the United States.

An agreement was finally reached and signed by Egyptian and Israeli officers on November 11. The agreement was not popular among the Egyptian military, who believed that they could have pushed Israeli forces back further, had the fighting continued. Sadat was satisfied, however. The treaty stipulated that the majority of Israeli forces would withdraw from positions 22 miles (35 kilometers) east of the Suez Canal. Sadat was willing to concede Israeli occupation of portions of the Sinai in order to reserve it for future negotiations.

Sadat's decision to sign the agreement that was largely negotiated by Kissinger spelled an end to the relationship between Egypt and the Soviet Union. Sadat's popularity in other Arab nations was enormous, however.

Anwar Sadat viewed his ability to reopen the Suez Canal in June 1975 as one of the highlights of his presidency, and it was accomplished with U.S. assistance. The canal still needed to be deepened so that larger ships could pass through, and mines had to be cleared from it. Those who lived in the Canal Zone needed to be guaranteed a certain amount of security—they had lived as refugees for many years, and the region of the Suez Canal was still within range of Israeli artillery.

Despite the progress made, Sadat was frustrated at the slow pace of negotiations aimed at resolving the Middle East crisis. He knew that something more than a step-by-step process was needed. Leadership in the United States and Israel had changed. He wanted a more comprehensive agreement, one that could be negotiated and settled before power again changed hands.

When Jimmy Carter was elected president of the United States in 1976, Sadat traveled to the United States to meet with him. He felt comfortable with the American leader, believing him to be, at heart, "a farmer like me."[37]

Sadat outlined his proposals to Carter. He had big ideas and was willing to make concessions and to negotiate. Sadat

U.S. President Jimmy Carter is pictured above. When Carter was elected in 1976, Anwar Sadat traveled to the United States to meet with him. The two leaders would develop a good working relationship, and Carter would later prove integral to the signing of the peace accords between Israel and Egypt.

was facing domestic problems, as well: The economy in Egypt continued to struggle. Food prices rose dramatically, and riots broke out in Alexandria and Cairo. Martial law was required in order for calm to be restored.

In addition to domestic issues, Sadat was also facing international problems. Israel was building up its military at a time when Egypt had no source of weapons. The Egyptian military was weakened, and no country was willing to re-arm Egypt.

As Sadat assessed the situation, he realized that it was his responsibility—his duty—to try to negotiate a peaceful solution directly with Israel in order to spare future generations the suffering he and his people had known.[38]

Sadat's ideas began to crystallize after a meeting in Romania with its president, Nicolae Ceausescu. Ceausescu told Sadat that he had spent eight hours meeting with the newly elected Israeli leader, Menachem Begin. "Begin wants a solution," Ceausescu assured Sadat. "He wants peace."[39]

FROM OPPOSITION TO POWER

In August 1970, Begin had stepped down from his role in the coalition government and returned to his role as leading spokesman for the opposition. He focused increasingly, though, on peace. Regardless of his concerns for peace, however, Begin was uncompromising on the issue of division of what he viewed as absolute Israeli land. He warned the United States that the creation of a Palestinian state on Israeli soil would provide the Soviets with a base in the Middle East.

The October War was a shock to Begin and to the entire Israeli political system. Public dissatisfaction with the handling of the war would eventually make way Begin's rise to power. Israel's leader, Golda Meir, resigned. Conflicts soon emerged between her successor, Yitzhak Rabin, and two members of his cabinet, Defense Minister Shimon Peres and Foreign Minister Yigal Allon.

Charges of corruption and bribery were leveled against prominent figures in their political party (the Labor Party).

Begin stepped into this power vacuum. He had opposed the agreement negotiated by Kissinger between Israel and Egypt, and he spoke out forcefully against any plans for Israeli withdrawal from the Sinai. His Herut Party joined forces with other nationalistic and socialistic political parties eager to challenge the ruling Labor Party. They formed a coalition party known as Likud.

Begin held meetings at his simple Tel Aviv apartment. His modest lifestyle, at a time when charges of corruption were being leveled at other public officials, increased Begin's popularity.

As the 1977 election campaign was underway, Begin collapsed with a heart attack. It was a bad blow for Begin's campaign, as voters might not support a candidate whose health was poor.

Voters were also concerned about Begin's history of outspoken criticism of any attempt to negotiate away what he considered Israeli territory. His belligerence, his strident views, and his violent past were all well known to students of Israeli politics.

Begin's skillful political campaign helped set many of these concerns to rest. In a debate with the Labor Party candidate, Shimon Peres, Begin seemed relaxed and polite, whereas Peres was far more confrontational. Campaign ads emphasized Begin as a family man who enjoyed spending time with his grandchildren. Voters were reminded of his honesty and integrity.

On May 17, 1977, the election results were announced. The Likud Party had won. Menachem Begin was the new leader of Israel. On election night, a television reporter congratulated Begin, noting, "It's the biggest moment of your life, isn't it?"

"Oh no," Begin replied. "There were bigger in the underground, in the war for Israel's independence."[40]

Begin had built his political career on an absolute refusal to compromise one inch of Israeli territory. Six months after his election, he would welcome to Tel Aviv the leader of a country Israel had fought for 30 years.

CHAPTER 8

Peace Negotiations

On November 9, 1977, Anwar Sadat stood before the Egyptian Parliament and announced that he was prepared to go to Israel to pursue peace negotiations. The world was stunned by this announcement. Many believed that Sadat was making an empty promise. For about 30 years, Israel had been at war with the Arab world, and many viewed Egypt as Israel's greatest enemy.

Begin publicly responded that he would be willing to meet face to face with Egypt's leader. On November 16, Sadat received, via the American ambassador, a formal written invitation from Begin, inviting Sadat to Israel.

It was clear that a historic opportunity had presented itself. Little time was wasted on preparations; 10 days after Sadat's speech in front of the parliament, his plane was touching down at Ben-Gurion International Airport outside Tel Aviv. An international audience witnessed the historic arrival on television. As Sadat emerged from the plane, he was greeted by a large banner with the words "Welcome President Sadat" printed in Hebrew, Arabic, and English.[41]

Begin stepped forward, accompanied by Israel's president, Ephraim Katzir, and the three men shook hands. They stood at attention as the Israeli military band played the Egyptian and Israeli national anthems. Then Sadat was introduced to many Israeli leaders, including former prime ministers Yitzhak Rabin and Golda Meir, and men who led the Israeli military when Egypt launched its attack in 1973, including Moshe Dayan and former general Ariel Sharon.

Sadat joked with Ariel Sharon, "If you attempt to cross to the West Bank again, I'll put you in jail!"

"Oh no," Sharon replied. "I'm Minister of Culture now!"[42]

It is perhaps true that only Begin and Sadat had the strength and authority within their own countries to make this historic gesture. These two leaders had built their careers on their determination to ensure their nation's independence. They demonstrated their willingness to do whatever was necessary, including wage war, to preserve the integrity of their nations. Sadat's visit to Israel lasted only 44 hours, but during that brief time, many extraordinary moments were witnessed.

Begin and Sadat had a private meeting. The morning after his arrival, Sadat traveled to the Old City of Jerusalem to the Al-Aqsa Mosque, one of the holiest sites in the Muslim faith, where he prayed. In the afternoon, Sadat spoke before the Knesset, the Israeli parliament. His speech electrified the audience. Sadat noted that he had not consulted with any other Arab leaders before his visit. He emphasized the plight of the Palestinian people and said that he made this visit on their behalf, as well as on behalf of the Egyptian people. He said that he was not in Israel to "forge a unilateral agreement between Egypt and Israel,"[43] but that he wished to live in peace with Israel, to accept it as a reality, and to allow it whatever guarantees it needed for its security. Sadat also noted, however, that Israel must withdraw from all Arab territories occupied in 1967, including the Arab section of Jerusalem.

In November 1977, Anwar Sadat made his first, historic visit to Israel. Above, Sadat and Begin shake hands after Sadat addressed the Knesset. During his trip, Sadat also met with Begin privately and visited the Al-Aqsa mosque in Jerusalem.

Begin responded with an outstretched hand. He noted Sadat's courage in traveling to Israel and called for negotiations to bring about "real peace with complete reconciliation between Jewish and Arab peoples."[44]

Inspired by Sadat's gesture, Begin announced his willingness to negotiate with all of Israel's Arab neighbors. He invited Syria's President Hafez Assad and Jordan's King Hussein to come to Israel as well.

It was an amazing moment, one celebrated both in Israel and Egypt. When Sadat returned home, he was given a hero's welcome. His gesture was not celebrated throughout the Arab world, however. The Syrian president declared that November 19, the day Sadat traveled to Jerusalem, should be designated a national day of mourning. Libya's leader, Muammar Qaddafi, closed his airports and docks to Egyptian traffic.[45]

Sadat later said that the purpose of his trip to Jerusalem was to "break the vicious cycle within which we had been caught up for years."[46] This goal was achieved, at least temporarily. Sadat's hopes for Israel's withdrawal from the Sinai and the creation of a Palestinian state were disappointed, however.

Begin traveled to Ismailia, Egypt, in December 1977, but both Begin and Sadat were disappointed with the outcome of that meeting. Begin had expected to be welcomed to the Egyptian capital of Cairo and to be met with great pomp. Sadat had expected Begin to arrive with specific details in response to Sadat's proposals in Jerusalem. The meeting ended without any great success.

ENTER THE AMERICANS

American President Jimmy Carter had met with both Sadat and Begin while the two men were reaching out to each other. Carter believed that an historic opportunity was slipping away, one that could be resolved with the intervention of a third party. He wanted the United States to be that third party, to protect American interests in the region and to help ensure a solution to the Palestinian problem.

In early meetings, Carter felt much more comfortable with Sadat than with Begin.[47] He was determined to shepherd the two men to a peace agreement, however, so he invited them both to a conference at the presidential retreat at Camp David.

By the time the three leaders gathered at Camp David in September 1978, it was uncertain whether an agreement could be reached. During the 13 days of the conference, Begin and Sadat would occasionally take walks on the paths that wound through the mountains around the retreat. For the most part, though, it was Carter who kept the two men focused on achieving a resolution, to reach a compromise. Carter's involvement

Influences on the Peacemaker

Both Begin and Sadat publicly—and in their Nobel acceptance speeches—acknowledged the important role U.S. President Jimmy Carter played in the Camp David accords and the signing of the Egypt–Israeli peace treaty. Carter, the thirty-ninth president of the United States, was born in 1924 in the farming community of Plains, Georgia. He was a graduate of the U.S. Naval Academy, served in both the Atlantic and Pacific fleets, and rose to the rank of lieutenant. He was chosen to serve in the nuclear submarine program, and he pursued graduate studies in nuclear physics and reactor technology.

Carter married in 1946. He resigned his naval commission in 1953, following the death of his father, and moved back to Georgia to manage the family farm. He became involved in local politics, and in 1962 was elected to the Georgia Senate. He ran for governor in 1966 and lost, but he was elected and became governor of Georgia in 1971.

Carter announced his candidacy for president in 1974. After the turmoil of Watergate, American voters were eager for a Washington outsider, someone who represented a change from the Nixon years. The "peanut farmer" from Georgia was elected president in 1976.

The Camp David Accords would become one of the high points of Carter's presidency. His administration struggled, however, as the nation battled an energy embargo, and he was unable to resolve the crisis that followed the seizure of American hostages at the U.S. embassy in Iran. Carter served only one term as president.

After leaving the presidency, Carter became a champion for issues involving human rights and conflict resolution. In addition to work for Habitat for Humanity, Carter was prominently involved in efforts to resolve conflicts in numerous troubled regions of the world, including Ethiopia, North Korea, Liberia, Haiti, Sudan, and Bosnia. He founded the nonprofit Carter Center, which addresses public policy issues, and authored several best-selling works of nonfiction and fiction. He was awarded the Nobel Peace Prize for these and other efforts in 2002.

Israeli Prime Minister Menachem Begin (left), U.S. President Jimmy Carter (center), and Anwar Sadat (right), president of Egypt, pose for a photograph at Camp David, where they met to negotiate a new peace agreement between Israel and Egypt.

added additional pressure—both men were eager to maintain good relations with the United States and to preserve the strong public opinion that supported their efforts at reaching a peaceful solution to the conflict.

The meeting ended with the signing of the Camp David Accords at the White House on September 17, 1978. The accords granted a commitment from Israel to withdraw from the Sinai within three years. Egypt committed to normalize relations with Israel. The two nations agreed to reach a "just, comprehensive, and durable settlement of the Middle East conflict through the conclusion of peace treaties."[48] The rights of the Palestinian people were recognized, and a process was to be set up to implement "full autonomy" within five years. The idea of "autonomy" was an important concept for Begin. It did not give the Palestinians the right to an independent state, which would have meant ceding part of what Begin viewed as Israeli land, nor did it give them citizenship in Israel. Instead, it provided them with the right of self-rule. Egypt agreed to end its economic boycott of Israel and to grant Israeli ships access to the Suez Canal.

Many points were left vague by the accords. There was no specific commitment for full Israeli withdrawal from the West Bank or Gaza. There was no deadline by which full autonomy for the Palestinians would occur. There was no mention of withdrawing or halting Israeli settlements in the disputed territories, nor was there a discussion of the status of Jerusalem.

Both men soon came under harsh criticism within their own countries (and in Sadat's case, throughout the Arab world) for what they had agreed to and for what had not been included. President Carter, however, was determined to finalize—and formalize—what had been agreed to at the Camp David meetings. On March 26, 1979, Sadat and Begin met once more at the White House, this time to sign the Egyptian–Israeli Peace Treaty. President Carter witnessed the signing.

NOBEL PEACE PRIZE

The historic steps taken toward peace by Sadat and Begin were rewarded in 1978 with the announcement that the two men had been chosen as recipients of the Nobel Peace Prize. In the presentation speech, Aase Lionaes, Chair of the Norwegian Nobel Committee, noted that the men were chosen "for their contribution to the two frame agreements on peace in the Middle East, and on peace between Egypt and Israel, which were signed at Camp David on September 17, 1978."[49]

Lionaes noted that the peace agreement was the first between Egypt and Israel in some 3,000 years, since the days of King Solomon and the Egyptian pharaohs. She stated:

Above, Sadat, Carter, and Begin share a three-way handshake after sign-ing the official Egyptian–Israeli peace treaty on the White House lawn in Washington, D.C., on March 26, 1979.

Men of good will all over the world will now follow in their thoughts these two prize-winners in their endeavours to solve this great task of establishing peace. . . . May I express the hope that this Nobel Peace Prize ceremony, enacted in our small and wintry country, tucked away near the Arctic Circle, may provide an enduring reminder to the world that it was here that representatives of Egypt and Israel shook hands as they celebrated the greatest of all victories—conciliation and lasting peace based on respect for human rights and human dignity.[50]

The two leaders learned that they had been awarded the prize in late October. They congratulated each other by telephone. Sadat chose not to attend the ceremony and, instead, sent his special assistant, Sayed Marei, to accept the award on his behalf. Marei charmed the Norwegians by thanking them for their "warm reception," as he stood at the Oslo airport in temperatures of −18°C (about 0°F).[51] Begin chose to attend the ceremony, and he and his wife Aliza traveled to Norway, where they were entertained by the Norwegian king, Olav V, at the royal palace.

The award sparked controversy, particularly among those who suggested that it was premature, and that it expressed the hopes of the Nobel Committee that the Camp David Accords might lead to peace in the Middle East without any real evidence that peace had been achieved. Protestors marched outside the Nobel ceremonies, chanting, "Begin is a terrorist! Support the PLO!"[52]

On December 10, 1978, the traditional Nobel Lectures (speeches by the prizewinners) were presented. Sadat's comments were delivered by Sayed Marei. The speech acknowledged the important contribution of Jimmy Carter and restated Sadat's pledge to pursue

> the road to peace. . . . We have now come . . . in the peace process, to a moment of truth which requires each one of us to take a new look at the situation. . . . The ideal is the greatest one in the history of man, and we have accepted the challenge to translate it from a cherished hope into a living reality, and to win through vision and imagination, the hearts and minds of our peoples and enable them to look beyond the unhappy past.[53]

Begin, in his lecture, noted that the prize was not his to claim; it belonged instead,

> to my people—the ancient people and renaissant nation that came back in love and devotion to the land of its ancestors after centuries of homelessness and persecution. This prestigious recognition is due to this people because they suffered so much, because they lost so many, because they love peace

and want it with all their hearts for themselves and for their neighbors.[54]

Begin would later donate his half of the prize money—roughly $85,000—to an Israeli foundation that provided funding for student volunteers working with underprivileged children.

CHAPTER 9

A Premature Prize

The signing of the Camp David Accords and the Egypt–Israeli peace treaty provided Sadat with the Nobel Peace Prize and tremendous acclaim in the West. At home, and among his fellow Arab leaders, however, the negotiations prompted tremendous criticism. Much of it focused on the fact that the agreements provided no resolution for the Palestinian people.

Many Arab nations broke diplomatic relations with Egypt. Others chose to impose a boycott on Egyptian goods. The headquarters of the Arab League, which had long been in Cairo, was moved to Tunis. Egyptian newspapers and magazines were banned in much of the Arab world. The Palestine Liberation Organization (PLO), a militant group led by Yasir Arafat, protested the treaty with bombs and attempted attacks against the Egyptian and Israeli embassies in Turkey and Cyprus.

To make matters worse, Sadat felt that Begin was not enacting the kinds of sweeping changes that might make peace a reality. Negotiations between the two sides failed to resolve the question

Yasir Arafat is pictured above in a photograph from 1981. At the time of the Camp David Peace Accords, Arafat was the leader of the PLO, which staunchly opposed the peace accords. He led the PLO in protesting the treaty with bombs and attempted attacks against the Egyptian and Israeli embassies in Turkey and Cyprus.

of when the Palestinians might achieve autonomy. Settlement continued in the West Bank territories, without any attempts by Begin to put a stop to it.

Both men faced their own internal crises. Some within Begin's own party questioned his health and vigor, and suggested that he should retire. Begin was facing an election in 1981. His party had suffered setbacks in the 1979 elections, and it was not clear whether Begin the peacemaker had won popular support for his policies.

Then came the news that Iraqi president Saddam Hussein, a man Begin described as "the Butcher of Baghdad,"[55] was build-

History of the Nobel Peace Prize

The awarding of an annual prize for peace was the idea of the scientist and inventor Alfred Nobel, who was born in Stockholm, Sweden, on October 21, 1833. When Nobel died in 1896, his will specified that a significant portion of his fortune should be dedicated to the creation of five prizes, including one for peace. According to Nobel's will, the prize for peace was to be given to the person who had done "the most or best work for fraternity between nations, for the abolition or reduction of standing armies and for the holding of peace congresses." Nobel also specified that unlike the other prizes, which were to be awarded by Swedish committees, the prize for peace was to be awarded by a committee of five people elected by the Norwegian *Storting* (Parliament).

The first Nobel Peace Prize was awarded in 1901 to joint recipients Frédéric Passy and Jean Henry Dunant. Passy was leader of the French peace movement, and main organizer of the first Universal Peace Congress. Dunant was the founder of the International Red Cross.

Over the years, organizations as well as individuals have been awarded the Nobel Peace Prize. The first organization to receive the prize was the Institute for International Law, honored in 1904 for its efforts to formulate the general principles that would form the sci-

ing a nuclear reactor in the Iraqi town of Osirak. Begin viewed the prospect of an Iraq with nuclear capability as a direct threat to Israel. He announced to his cabinet, "There will be no other Holocaust in this century."[56]

On June 7, 1981, Israeli planes dropped 16 iron bombs on the nuclear reactor. All were direct hits. The bombing proved a popular action with Israeli voters. Begin had been acclaimed following the Camp David negotiations, but his actions against Iraq proved that the peace negotiator would also stand tough against Arab nations when necessary. In the 1981 elections, Begin's party was again reelected.

ence of international law. The International Committee of the Red Cross received the prize twice—in 1917 and 1944, for its efforts to promote international solidarity and brotherhood in the midst of war. The Office of the United Nations High Commissioner for Refugees received the prize in 1954; other organizations to receive the prize include the United Nations Children's Fund (UNICEF) in 1965, the Friends Service Council in Britain/American Friends Service Committee (1947), United Nations Peacekeeping Forces (1988), International Physicians for the Prevention of Nuclear War (1985), and Médécins sans Frontières (Doctors without Borders) in 1999.

Over the years, the award has highlighted the achievements of men and women from many different nations who represent widely varying backgrounds and experiences. It is interesting to note that one of the people most closely identified with nonviolence, Mohandas Gandhi of India, never received the Nobel Peace Prize, despite five nominations. Jimmy Carter, who was instrumentally involved in the Camp David negotiations, was not included with Anwar Sadat and Menachem Begin in the 1978 Peace Prize. He would wait another 24 years—until 2002—for his Nobel Peace Prize, awarded according to the Nobel committee "for his untiring effort to find peaceful solutions to international conflicts," including the conflict in the Middle East.

DOMESTIC TROUBLE

In the aftermath of the Camp David negotiations, Sadat struggled to hold onto the popular acclaim that had greeted him after his historic visit to Jerusalem. Sadat's accomplishments in foreign policy were clear, but domestically, Egypt was in many ways facing the same problems it had faced when Sadat first came to office. Unemployment was high, and the vast majority of Egyptians were not well educated, leaving nearly 75 percent illiterate.[57] The government was inefficient. Population growth was also skyrocketing.

As more and more people crowded into Egypt's cities, resources were in increasingly short supply. The government struggled to provide its people with water, electricity, and housing. Traffic clogged the streets, and blackouts were a fact of life in Cairo. Land available for farming was increasingly limited, which forced Egypt to import much of its food.

Sadat had formed a firm personal relationship with President Carter, but when Carter was defeated in the 1980 presidential elections, Sadat struggled to build a similar relationship with the new president, Ronald Reagan.

The decision by Begin to bomb the Iraqi nuclear reactor outraged Sadat. Many in the Arab world assumed that Sadat had been informed by Begin of the attack in advance, making him somehow complicit in the decision. A year earlier, the Israeli Knesset had added another challenge to the peace process, when it announced that Jerusalem was the "united and indivisible capital of Israel." This was viewed as a violation of the agreements that had once specified Jerusalem as a divided city in acknowledgment of its sacred nature to both Jews and Muslims.

"Whose side are they on?" Sadat complained to his wife. "Instead of working with me, the Israelis are putting me in one corner after another. It is as if they have joined with the Arabs to fight against Egypt and peace."[58]

Fundamentalist imams (Muslim religious leaders) in Egypt began to preach a message that urged their followers to reclaim

Jerusalem, using force if necessary. Their message promoting a far more conservative brand of Islam began to attract converts, who protested on university campuses against coeducation, Western music, and classes held during the times for prayer.

Civil war threatened, and Sadat attempted to appease the fundamentalists with small steps. He offered classes in the Koran in government schools, allocated money for the construction of mosques in poor Cairo neighborhoods, and decreed a pause in television programming during the five-times-a-day call to prayer. Violent clashes broke out between Muslims and Coptic Christians. Religion was suddenly becoming a divisive issue in Cairo neighborhoods.

Sadat once asked his wife, "What is the use of democracy if I put everyone opposed to me in prison?"[59]

In September 1981, shortly after returning from a meeting in the United States with President Reagan, Sadat once again attempted to restore order in his country. Police were ordered to take into custody anyone connected with the religious violence. Nearly 1,500 people were arrested, including fundamentalist priests. Sadat outlawed the wearing of the *niqab* (the garment that totally covered a woman's body except her eyes) on college campuses, where fundamentalist groups had been attempting to pressure women into wearing it.

Sadat decided that he would step down from the presidency in April 1982. It would be the date when Israeli troops would complete their withdrawal from the Sinai and when the land would officially once more become Egyptian territory.

With the detention of so many who had criticized his regime, Sadat faced new charges of being a dictator and of claiming to love democracy but muzzling those who did not agree with his policies. Sadat also faced constant personal threats.

The former leader began to discuss with his wife, Jehan, his sense that he had fulfilled a mission. He spoke of premonitions that his life would not last long, and he told her where he wished to be buried.

AN END TO PEACEMAKING

On October 6, 1981, Anwar Sadat participated in the annual celebrations that marked the anniversary of Egypt's victory over Israel. It had been eight years since Sadat gave the orders that sent Egyptian troops into battle. On that anniversary, Sadat was dressed in his military uniform as he sat in the reviewing stand and watched the military parade. Seated nearby were his wife, Jehan, and Sadat's four grandchildren.

As the military vehicles paraded past and jets did aerobatics overhead, an army truck suddenly pulled out of formation and stopped in front of the reviewing stand. Three men rushed toward the stands holding machine guns. A grenade exploded and smoke filled the air, followed by the reports of gunfire.

When the gunfire ended, Anwar Sadat was dead. Muslim fundamentalists operating within the military had killed him. They fired upon Sadat for at least a minute before security forces returned fire, killing not only the Egyptian leader but also killing or injuring several other diplomats. "Negligence killed my husband," Jehan Sadat wrote in her memoirs:

> Carelessness killed my husband. Anwar's own affection for the armed forces, his belief that they could not be infiltrated by the Muslim fanatics, helped kill my husband. . . . "This is inconceivable," were Anwar's last words to [Vice President] Husni Mubarak as the members of his own Army ran toward him, their machine guns spitting death.[60]

The conflict that had marked Sadat's attempt to bring peace to the Middle East was reflected in the reaction to his death. President Reagan condemned the attack that had killed Sadat, noting, "America has lost a great friend, the world has lost a great statesman, and mankind has lost a champion of peace."[61]

Radio stations in the Libyan capital of Tripoli, however, broadcast contrary messages that "every tyrant has an end," as thousands took to the streets to celebrate. One PLO official said,

During the celebrations of October 6, 1981, an army truck suddenly pulled out of formation and stopped in front of the reviewing stand where Anwar Sadat was seated. A grenade exploded and shots were fired, killing Sadat. This photograph was taken moments after the explosion.

"We were expecting this end of President Sadat because we are sure he was against the interests of his people, the Arab nations and the Palestinian people."[62] Sadat's funeral was attended by three former U.S. presidents, by Prince Charles of England, and by leaders from Germany, France, and the Soviet Union. Leaders from Africa and representatives of European royalty all attended. Still, the Arab nations refused to attend the funeral of the man they had once hailed for his victory over Israel. Only the presidents of Sudan and Somalia came to pay their respects.

Jehan Sadat documented her confrontation with some of the Arab leaders following the funeral, in which she asked why they had not attended. One replied, "Because Begin attended, and I would not walk in the same funeral procession as the Prime Minister of Israel."[63]

FAREWELL TO BEGIN

The tentative steps toward peace taken by Sadat and Begin would soon be nothing more than a memory. In December 1981, Begin's government annexed the Golan Heights territory, a strategically important stretch of land that contained thousands of Jewish settlers but was scheduled to be returned to Syria.

In June 1982, Israel launched a ground, sea, and air assault on Lebanon, initially targeting the Palestinian strongholds there that had been waging a guerilla war against Israel. Soon, however, Israeli tanks surrounded the Lebanese capital of Beirut. Israel's defense minister, Ariel Sharon, soon moved beyond the initial goal of eliminating the PLO presence in southern Lebanon. As his troops moved north, deeper into Lebanon, they incurred thousands of civilian casualties and left tens of thousands of Lebanese homeless.

Israeli public opinion quickly turned against Begin and Sharon. What had initially been described as an effort to stamp out PLO attacks on Israeli soil quickly became another Arab–Israeli war. President Reagan also intervened, calling on Begin to bring an end to the war that was killing so many innocent civilians and destroying their capital. In the course of a heated phone conversation, Reagan referred to the events in Lebanon as a "holocaust." Begin replied that he, not the U.S. president, knew what that word meant.[64]

The bombing of Beirut was finally halted, and Israeli troops began to plan their withdrawal. The Lebanese elected a new president, Bachir Gemayel, but on September 14, the president-elect was assassinated by a bomb blast, later attributed to the Syrian National Party. This would spark a disastrous chain of events. A group of Lebanese militia, with the support of the Israeli army, entered two Palestinian refugee camps; they claimed their goal was to hunt out anyone who might have been involved in the assassination. Instead, though, the militia murdered the Palestinian men, women, and children in the camps. By the time they were finished, hundreds were dead.

The international community was outraged when word of the massacre leaked out. The Israeli public was equally outraged.

On September 29, nearly 400,000 Israelis (about 10 percent of the entire population of the nation) gathered in Tel Aviv in a mass rally, demanding punishment for those responsible for the massacre. Begin reluctantly agreed, and a commission was appointed to investigate.

Testifying before the commission two months after the massacre, Begin seemed disorganized and out of touch. He could not recall key events, nor could he consistently understand what his questioners were asking of him.

The bulk of the blame for the events in Lebanon fell on Defense Minister Ariel Sharon, but Begin, too, was criticized by the commission. One commenter noted, "The Prime Minister's lack of involvement in the entire matter casts on him a certain degree of responsibility."[65]

Sharon was forced to resign from his position as defense minister. He remained in Begin's cabinet, however, as a minister without portfolio.

In November 1981, 68-year-old Begin fell and fractured his femur, the large thigh bone extending from the pelvis to the knee. Begin remained in the hospital for nearly three weeks and spent the following months in severe pain. He initially used a wheelchair to maneuver, then a cane. Because sitting at the desk was painful, he was forced to work from a sofa. Begin used the injury as a prop, demonstrating his determination with phrases like, "I broke my leg, but my knee is not bent."[66]

On November 13, 1982, Begin's beloved wife, Aliza, died after many years of deteriorating health and chronic asthma. The couple had been married for 43 years. Her death deeply affected Begin.

Begin announced to his cabinet on August 28, 1983, that he intended to resign, stating, "I feel I cannot carry on shouldering my responsibilities, with things as they are, the way I would like to and the way I ought to."[67] Yitzhak Shamir was chosen as Begin's successor, and on September 15, Begin formally stepped down and retired from public life.

President Jimmy Carter waves as he and his wife, Begin and his wife (at left), and Sadat and his wife (at right), pause before being seated at a White House state dinner, celebrating the signing of the peace treaty between Egypt and Israel.

Menachem Begin died on March 9, 1992, of heart failure. He was 79 years old. In keeping with his wishes, he was buried on Jerusalem's Mount of Olives in a simple religious ceremony.

LEGACY OF THE PEACEMAKERS

The peace that both Begin and Sadat had hoped to achieve has proved elusive. The regions of the West Bank, Gaza, and Sinai continue to serve as flashpoints in the region. The question of the status of the Palestinian people has not yet been completely answered. Lebanon remains a country marked by conflict and a launching point for attacks against Israel.

On September 13, 1993, Israeli Prime Minister Yitzhak Rabin and the leader of the Palestine Liberation Organization, Yasir Arafat, held a historic meeting brokered by U.S. President Bill Clinton. Both men signed an agreement that required the PLO to recognize Israel's right to exist and to cease terrorist activities. It also required Israel to recognize the PLO as the official representative of the Palestine people and to begin a rapid withdrawal of Israeli armed forces from the occupied territories. In addition, the agreement spelled out the steps by which the region would move toward independence.

The agreement would cost Arafat much-needed Arab support. It would cost Rabin his life. At a rally held in Tel Aviv on November 4, 1995, to celebrate the ongoing peace process, Rabin was assassinated by a right-wing Jewish fundamentalist. Subsequent attempts at peace negotiations have broken down over the question of Jewish settlements in the West Bank and Gaza, over the status of Jerusalem, and over the question of Palestinian rights.

Israel continues to fight to preserve its security and to guarantee its right to the independence first declared in May 1948. In that declaration of independence, however, Israel declared that one of its principal goals was peaceful cooperation with the Arabs of Israel and neighboring Arab nations in a common effort to promote the advancement of the entire Middle East. Fulfillment of this goal also remains elusive.

In one of his final interviews, Anwar Sadat was asked by a reporter what he would wish for if he was granted three wishes. Sadat replied, "One, peace in the Middle East. Two, peace in the Middle East. Three, peace in the Middle East."[68]

Sadat's legacy in Egypt is still uncertain. The economic prosperity he had hoped to bring to his country has not yet materialized. Arab–Israeli negotiations failed to produce a lasting peace, despite the promise of Sadat's successor, Hosni Mubarak, to support the Camp David Accords and follow Sadat's plans for peace. Sadat did succeed in building a strong relationship with the United States, though—one that resulted in billions of dollars of aid and

U.S. President Bill Clinton presides over White House ceremonies marking the signing of the peace accord between Israel and the Palestinians, with Israeli Prime Minister Yitzhak Rabin, left, and PLO chairman Yasir Arafat, right, in Washington, September 13, 1993.

a strengthened military. This strong military, perhaps ironically, has produced its own peace. Sadat also ensured that Egypt was a key player in any negotiations involving Arab interests.

The Camp David Accords represented a beginning, rather than any conclusive end to violence. They were historic simply for what they represented—an opportunity for an Israeli leader and an Arab leader to sit down and discuss how peace might be achieved in the future, rather than the achievement of any concrete or lasting accomplishments in the present.

Nonetheless, historic points were negotiated at Camp David—points that represent an important part of the legacies of Begin and Sadat. The Sinai was returned to Egypt. Diplomatic relations were established between Egypt and Israel. A framework was drafted to address the question of Palestinian self-governance. President Jimmy Carter would also be awarded his own Nobel Peace Prize in 2002 in part for his important role in those negotiations and what he accomplished at Camp David.

Sadat's legacy is also full of ironies. He first built a reputation as the man who led the 1973 attack against Israel, and his victory was celebrated by Arabs as a significant turning point in the ongoing conflict between Israel and the Arab world. Several years later, he would reach out to Israel in a gesture that would launch the peace process, a move celebrated by an international audience as a sign that the conflict between Israel and the Arab world might finally be coming to an end.

Begin, too, has a legacy of contradictions. He was the first Israeli leader to sign a peace treaty with an Arab nation. His resistance to ceding any portion of Israeli territory, however, made it nearly impossible for future Israeli governments to return the West Bank and Gaza Strip to Arab control.

In his historic speech before the Israeli Knesset on November 20, 1977, Sadat shared his dream of a future where peace might become a reality. He declared:

> Any life that is lost in war is a human life, be it that of an Arab or an Israeli. A wife who becomes a widow is a human being entitled to a happy family life, whether she be an Arab or an Israeli. Innocent children who are deprived of the care and compassion of their parents are ours. They are ours, be they living on Arab or Israeli land. They command our full responsibility to afford them a comfortable life today and tomorrow.[69]

Nobel Lecture of Menachem Begin
Delivered on December 10, 1978

Your Majesty, Your Royal Highnesses, Your Excellencies, Madame Chairlady and Members of the Nobel Prize Committee, Mr. Marei, representative of the President of Egypt, Ladies and Gentlemen.

I ask for permission first to pay tribute to Golda Meir, my predecessor, a great leader and Prime Minister, who strove with all her heart to achieve peace between Israel and her neighbors. Her blessed memory will live forever in the hearts of the Jewish people and of all peace-loving nations.

I have come from the Land of Israel, the land of Zion and Jerusalem, and here I stand in humility and with pride as a son of the Jewish people, as one of the generation of the Holocaust and Redemption.

The ancient Jewish people gave the world the vision of eternal peace, of universal disarmament, of abolishing the teaching and learning of war. Two Prophets, Yeshayahu Ben Amotz and Micha HaMorashti, having foreseen the spiritual unity of man under God—with His word coming forth from Jerusalem—gave the nations of the world the following vision expressed in identical terms:

"And they shall beat their swords into ploughshares and their spears into pruning hooks. Nation shall not lift up sword against nation; neither shall they learn war any more."

We mortals who believe in Divine Providence, when recalling those sacred prophecies, ask ourselves not whether, but when is this vision going to become reality? We remember the past; even in this century alone—and we know. We look around—and see. Millions of men of all nations are under arms. Intercontinental missiles deposited in the bowels of the earth or lying on the beds of oceans can destroy man and everything he has built. Not in Alfred Nobel's time, but in our own era, has mankind become capable of destroying itself and returning the earth to *Tohu Vevohu.* Under such circumstances, should we, can we, keep our faith in an eternal peace that will one day reign over mankind? Yes, we should and we can. Perhaps that very capability of total destruction of our little planet—achieved for the first time in the annals of mankind—will one day, God willing, become the origin, the cause and the prime mover for the elimination of all instruments of destruction from the face of the earth and ultimate peace, prayed for and yearned for by previous generations, will become the portion of all nations. Despite the tragedies and disappointments of the past, we must never forsake that vision, that human dream, that unshakeable faith.

Peace is the beauty of life. It is sunshine. It is the smile of a child, the love of a mother, the joy of a father, the togetherness of a family. It is the advancement of man, the victory of a just cause, the triumph of truth. Peace is all of these and more and more.

But in my generation, Ladies and Gentlemen, there was a time indescribable. Six million Jews—men, women, and children—a number larger than many a nation in Europe—were dragged to a wanton death and slaughtered methodically in the heart of the civilized continent. It was not a sudden outburst of human or rather inhuman cruelty that from time to time has happened in the history of mankind; it was a systematic process of extermination which unfolded before the eyes of the whole world for more than six years. Those who were doomed, deprived of their human dignity, starved, humiliated, led away, and ultimately turned into ashes, cried out for rescue—but in vain. Other than a few famous and unforgettable exceptions they were left alone to face the destroyer.

At such a time, unheard of since the first generation, the hour struck to rise and fight—for the dignity of man, for survival, for liberty, for every value of the human image a man has been endowed with by his Creator, for every known inalienable right he stands for and lives for. Indeed, there are days when to fight for a cause so absolutely just is the highest human command. Norway has known such days, and so have we. Only in honoring that command comes the *regeneration* of the concept of peace. You rise, you struggle, you make sacrifices to achieve and guarantee the prospect and hope of living in peace—for you and your people, for your children and their children.

Let it, however, be declared and known, stressed, and noted that fighters for freedom hate war. My friends and I learned this precept from Zeev Jabotinsky through his own example, and through the one he set for us from Giuseppe Garibaldi. Our brothers in spirit, wherever they dwell, learned it from *their* masters and teachers. This is our common maxim and belief—that if through your efforts and sacrifices you win liberty and with it the prospect of peace, then work for peace because there is no mission in life more sacred.

And so reborn Israel always strove for peace, yearned for it, made endless endeavors to achieve it. My colleagues and I have gone in the footsteps of our predecessors since the very first day we were called by our people to care for their future. We went any place, we looked for any avenue, we made any effort to bring about negotiations between Israel and its neighbors, negotiations without which peace remains an abstract desire.

We have labored long and hard to turn it into a reality— because of the blessings it holds for ourselves, our neighbors, the world. In peace, the Middle East, the ancient cradle of civilization, will become invigorated and transformed. Throughout its lands there will be freedom of movement of people, of ideas, of goods. Cooperation and development in agriculture will make the deserts blossom. Industry will bring the promise of a better life. Sources of water will be developed and the almost year-long sunshine will yet be harnessed for the common needs of all the nations. Yes, indeed, the Middle East, standing at the crossroads of the world, will become a peaceful center of international communication between East and West, North and South—a center of human advancement in every sphere of creative endeavor. This and more is what peace will bring to our region.

During the past year many efforts for peace were made and many significant events took place. The President of the Arab Republic of Egypt expressed his readiness to come to Jerusalem, the eternal capital of Israel, and to address our parliament, the Knesset. When that message reached me I, without delay or hesitation, extended to President Sadat on behalf of Israel, an invitation to visit our country. I told him: You will be received with respect and cordiality. And, indeed, so he was received, cordially and respectfully, by the people, by the parliament and by the government of our nation. We knew and learned that we have differences of opinion. But whenever we recall those days of Jerusalem we say, always, that they were shining, beautiful days of friendliness and understanding. It was in this same atmosphere that the meetings in Ismailya were conducted. In the spirit of the Nobel Prize tradition we gave to each other the most momentous pledge: No more war. No more bloodshed. We shall negotiate and reach agreement.

Admittedly, there were difficult times as well. Let nobody forget that we deal with a conflict of more than sixty years with its manifold tragedies. These, we must put behind us in order to establish friendship and make peace the beauty of our lives.

Many of the difficulties were overcome at Camp David where the President of the United States, Mr. Jimmy Carter, unforgettably invested unsparing effort, untiring energy and great devotion in the peace-making process. There, despite all the differences, we found solutions for problems, agreed on issues and the Framework for Peace was signed. With its signature, there was rejoicing in our countries and throughout the world. The path leading to peace was paved.

The phase that followed was the natural arduous negotiations to elaborate and conclude a peace treaty as we promised each other to do at Camp David. The delegations of both countries worked hard and have, I believe, produced a draft document that can serve, if and when signed and ratified, as a good treaty of peace between countries that decided to put an end to hostility and war and begin a new era of understanding and cooperation. Such a treaty can serve as the first indispensable step along the road towards a comprehensive peace in our region.

If, because of all these efforts, President Sadat and I have been awarded the Nobel Peace Prize, let me from this rostrum again congratulate him—as I did in a direct conversation between Jerusalem and Cairo a few weeks ago on the morrow of the announcement.

Now, it is I who must express gratitude from the bottom of my heart for the great honor you do me. But, Ladies and Gentlemen, before doing so, permit me to remind us all that today is an important anniversary—the thirtieth anniversary of the adoption of the Universal Declaration of Human Rights. Let us always remember the magnificently written words of its first Article. It expresses the essence of all the declarations of the rights of man and citizen written throughout history. It says:

"All human beings are born free and equal, in dignity and rights. They are endowed with reason and conscience and should act towards one another in a spirit of brotherhood."

Free women and men everywhere must wage an incessant campaign so that these human values become a generally recognized and practised reality. We must regretfully admit that in various parts of the world this is not yet the case. Without those values and human rights the real peace of which we dream is jeopardized.

For reasons self-understood, but which every man and woman of goodwill will accept, I must remind my honored listeners of my brethren and the prisoners who are deprived of one of their most basic rights: To go home. I speak about people of great courage who deserve not only the respect but also the moral support of the free world. I speak about people who, even from the depths of their suffering, repeat the age-long prayer:

Next year in Jerusalem.

The preservation and protection of human rights are indispensable to give peace of nations and individuals its real meaning.

Allow me, now, to turn to you, Madame President of the Nobel Peace Prize Committee and to all its members and say, thank you. I thank you for the great distinction. It does not, however, belong to me; it belongs to my people—the ancient people and renaissant nation that came back in love and devotion to the land of its ancestors after centuries of homelessness and persecution. This prestigious recognition is due to this people because they suffered so much, because they lost so many, because they love peace and want it with all their hearts for themselves and for their neighbors. On their behalf, I humbly accept the award and in their name I thank you from the bottom of my heart.

And may I express to His Majesty, the Ring, our deep gratitude for the gracious hospitality His Majesty, on this occasion, bestowed upon my wife and myself.

Your Majesty, Your Highnesses, Members of the Nobel Peace Prize Committee, Ladies and Gentlemen:

Seventy-seven years ago, the first Nobel Peace Prize was awarded. Jean Henri Dunant was its recipient. On December 10, 1901, the President of the Norwegian Parliament said:

"The Norwegian people have always demanded that their independence be respected. They have always been ready to defend it. But at the same time they have always had a keen desire and need for peace."

May I, Ladies and Gentlemen, on behalf of the people of Israel, respectfully subscribe to these true and noble words.

Thank you.

Source: "Menachem Begin: Nobel Lecture." Nobelprize.org. http://nobelprize .org/nobel_prizes/peace/laureates/1978/begin-lecture.html. © The Nobel Foundation 1978.

Nobel Lecture of Anwar Sadat
Delivered on December 10, 1978,
by Sayed Marei

Your Majesty, Your Royal Highnesses, Mr. Prime Minister of Israel, Madame Chairman and Members of The Nobel Peace Prize Committee, Excellencies, Distinguished Guests, Ladies and Gentlemen,

Peace be upon you. This is the traditional way in which, everyday, we greet one another. It reflects our deepest feelings and hopes. We always say it and we mean it.

Your Majesty, Ladies and Gentlemen,

The decision of the Nobel Prize Committee to bestow upon me the Peace Award has been received by the people of Egypt not only as an honor, but also as a confirmation of the universal recognition of our relentless efforts to achieve peace in an area in which God has chosen to bring to mankind, through Moses, Jesus, and Mohamed, His message of wisdom and light.

Your Majesty, Ladies and Gentlemen,

Recognition is due to a man of the highest integrity: President Jimmy Carter whose signal efforts to overcome obstacles in the way of peace deserves our keenest appreciation.

The road to peace is one which, throughout its history, which coincides with the dawn of human civilization, the people of Egypt have considered as befitting their genius, and their vocation. No people on earth have been more steadfastly faithful to the cause of peace, and none more attached to the principles of justice which constitute the cornerstone of any real and lasting peace.

Do I need to remind such an august and distinguished gathering, that the first recorded peace treaty in history was concluded more than three thousand years ago between Ramses the Great and Hattusilis, Prince of the Hittites, who resolved to establish "good peace and good brotherhood?"

And since then, through the ages, even when wars appeared as a necessary evil, the real genius of Egypt has been one of peace . . . and its ambition has been to build not to destroy, to create not to annihilate, to coexist not to eliminate. Thus, the land of Egypt has always been cherished by God Almighty: Moses lived there, Jesus fled to it from injustice and foreign domination, and the Holy Koran has blessed it. And Islam, which is the religion of justice, equality, and moral values, has added new dimensions to the eternal spirit of Egypt.

We have always realized that the qualities of chivalry, courage, faith, and discipline that were characteristic of a romantic concept of war, should, in an era where war has become only synonymous with devastation to all, be a means of enriching life, not generating death.

It is in this spirit that Alfred Nobel created the prize which bears his name and which is aimed at encouraging mankind to follow the path of peace, development, progress and prosperity.

Ladies and Gentlemen,

It is in the light of all this, that I embarked a year ago upon my initiative aimed at restoring peace in an area where man received the words of God.

Through me it was the eternal Egypt that was expressing itself: Let us put an end to wars, let us reshape life on the solid basis of equity and truth. And it is this call, which reflected the will of the Egyptian people, of the great majority of the Arab and Israeli peoples, and indeed of millions of men, women, and children around the world that you are today honoring. And these hundreds of millions will judge to what extent every responsible leader in the Middle East has responded to the hopes of mankind.

We have now come, in the peace process, to a moment of truth which requires each one of us to take a new look at the situation. I trust that you all know that when I made my historic trip to Jerusalem my aim was not to strike a deal as some politicians do.

I made my trip because I am convinced that we owe it to this generation and the generations to come, not to leave a stone unturned in our pursuit of peace. The ideal is the greatest one in the history of man, and we have accepted the challenge to translate it from a cherished hope into a living reality, and to win through vision and imagination, the hearts and minds of our peoples and enable them to look beyond the unhappy past.

Let me remind you of what I said in the Knesset, more than one year ago; I said:

"Let me tell you truthfully: Today we have a good chance for peace, an opportunity that cannot be repeated, if we are really serious in the quest for peace. If we throw or fritter away this chance, the curse of mankind and the curse of history will befall the one who plots against it."

I would like now, on this most solemn and moving occasion, to pledge again that we in Egypt—with the future rather than the past in mind—are determined to pursue in good faith, as we have always done, the road to peace, and to leave no avenue unexplored to reach this cherished goal, and to reconcile the sons of Ismail and the sons of Isaac. In renewing this pledge, which I hope that the other parties will also adhere to, I again repeat what I said in the Knesset more than a year ago:

"Any life lost in war is the life of a human being, irrespective of whether it is an Arab or an Israeli.

The wife who becomes widowed is a human being, entitled to live in a happy family, Arab or Israeli.

107

Innocent children, deprived of paternal care and sympathy are all our children, whether they live on Arab or Israeli soil and, we owe them the biggest responsibility of providing them with a happy present and bright future.

For the sake of all this, for the sake of protecting the lives of all our sons and brothers;

For our societies to produce in security and confidence;

For the development of man, his well-being and his right to share in an honorable life;

For our responsibility toward the coming generations;

For the smile of every child born on our land."

This is our conception of peace which I repeat today . . . The Day of Human Rights.

In the light of this let me share with you our conception of peace:

First, the true essence of peace which ensures its stability and durability, is justice. Any peace not built on justice and on the recognition of the rights of the peoples, would be a structure of sand which would crumble under the first blow.

The peace process comprises a beginning and steps towards an end. In reaching this end the process must achieve its projected goal. That goal is to bring security to the peoples of the area, and the Palestinians in particular, restoring to them all their right to a life of liberty and dignity. We are moving steadily towards this goal for all the peoples of the region. This is what I stand for. This is the letter and the spirit of Camp David.

Second, peace is indivisible. To endure, it should be comprehensive and involve all the parties in the conflict.

Third, peace and prosperity in our area are closely linked and interrelated. Our efforts should aim at achieving both, because it is as important to save man from death by destructive weapons, as it is not to abandon him to the evils of want and misery. And war is no cure for the problems of our area. And last, but not least, peace is a dynamic construction to which all should contribute, each adding a new brick. It goes far beyond a formal agreement or treaty, it transcends a word here or there. That is why it requires politicians who enjoy vision and imagination and who, beyond the present, look towards the future.

It is with this conviction, deeply rooted in our history and our faith, that the people of Egypt have embarked upon a major effort to achieve peace in the Middle East, an area of paramount importance to the whole world. We will spare no effort, we will not tire or despair, we will not lose faith, and we are confident that, in the end, our aim will be achieved.

I will ask you all to join me in a prayer that the day may soon come when peace will prevail, on the basis of justice and the recognition of the rights of all the peoples to shape their own life, to determine their own future, and to contribute to building a world of prosperity for all mankind.

Source: "Anwar Sadat: Nobel Lecture," Nobelprize.org. http://nobelprize .org/nobel_prizes/peace/laureates/1978/al-sadat-lecture.html. © The Nobel Foundation 1978.

1913 *August 16.* Menachem Begin is born in Brisk, Poland.

1918 *December 25.* Anwar Sadat is born in Mit Abul-Kum, Egypt.

1925 Sadat family moves to Cairo.

1926 Begin joins Zionist youth group Betar.

1931 Begin moves to Warsaw to enroll in law school; becomes employee of Betar.

1935 Begin is promoted to head Betar's Propaganda Department.

1936 Sadat enters Egypt's military academy.

1938 Sadat graduates from the military academy and begins his career as an officer.

1939 Begin is appointed head of Betar in Poland and marries Aliza Arnold. Germany invades Poland. Begin flees east into Lithuania.

1940 Begin is arrested by Soviet forces.

1941 Sadat first attempts military overthrow of government. Begin is released from prison and joins Free Polish Army.

1942 Sadat is arrested and thrown into prison. Begin arrives in Palestine with army unit.

1943 Begin named head of Irgun Zvai Leumi (IZL).

1944 Sadat escapes from prison. IZL publishes formal declaration of war against the British.

1945 Martial law is lifted in Egypt; Sadat resumes revolutionary activities.

1946 Sadat is imprisoned for participating in assassination of Egyptian finance minister.

1947 The UN votes to divide Palestine into two states, one Jewish and one Arab.

1948 Establishment of the state of Israel is announced; armies from Egypt, Jordan, Iraq, Syria, and Lebanon move into Palestine. Sadat is acquitted and released after 31 months in prison. Begin forms Herut political party.

1949 Sadat marries Jehan Raouf. War ends on February 24. Begin is elected to Knesset.

1950 Sadat's military commission is restored.

1952 Egyptian military overthrows government on July 22. Begin leads protest against decision to accept reparations from Germany.

1954 Nasser becomes leader of Egypt.

1956 *October 29.* Israel launches attack on Egypt, beginning Sinai-Suez War.

1966 Sadat visits the United States.

1967 Israel launches attack against Egypt on June 5; Gaza and Sinai territory are seized. Begin joins emergency government as minister without portfolio.

1969 Rogers Plan is announced.

1970 Nasser dies; Sadat becomes president of Egypt.

1972 Sadat expels Soviet military advisers. Begin leaves government and rejoins opposition.

1973 *October 6.* Sadat launches attack against Israel, marking the beginning of October War/Yom Kippur War.

1975 Sadat reopens Suez Canal.

1977 Begin becomes prime minister of Israel. Sadat visits Israel on November 19. Begin travels to Egypt in December.

1978 Begin and Sadat travel to Camp David to meet with U.S. President Jimmy Carter. Accords are signed on September 17. Begin and Sadat are awarded Nobel Peace Prize.

1979 *March 26.* Begin and Sadat sign Egyptian–Israeli Peace Treaty.

1981 Israeli planes bomb Iraqi nuclear reactor. Sadat is assassinated on October 6.

1982 Israel launches attack on Lebanon.

1983 Begin resigns.

1992 Begin dies on March 9.

NOTES

Chapter 1

1. "Egypt: War of Attrition and the October 1973 War," *Library of Congress Country Studies*. Available at www.memory.loc.gov.
2. Anwar Sadat, *In Search of Identity*. New York: Harper&Row, 1977, p. 261.
3. Ibid., p. 274.
4. "The Nobel Peace Prize 1978: Presentation Speech." Available at www.nobelprize.org.
5. Ibid.
6. Sadat, *In Search of Identity*, p. 274.

Chapter 2

7. Ibid., p. 11.
8. Ibid., p. 13.
9. Ibid., p. 14.
10. George Sullivan, *Sadat*. New York: Walker, 1981, p. 25.
11. Sadat, p. 17.

Chapter 3

12. Eitan Haber, *Menachem Begin*. New York: Delacorte, 1978, p. 20.
13. Ibid., p. 22.
14. Amos Perlmutter, *The Life and Times of Menachem Begin*. Garden City, N.Y.: Doubleday, 1987, p. 57.

Chapter 4

15. Menachem Begin, *White Nights: The Story of a Prisoner in Russia*. New York: Harper & Row, 1977, p. 40.

Chapter 5

16. Sadat, *In Search of Identity*, p. 73.
17. Ibid., p. 85.
18. Menachem Begin, *The Revolt*. New York: Nash, 1977, p. 41.
19. Haber, *Menachem Begin*, p. 98.
20. Begin, *The Revolt*, p. 59.
21. Haber, *Menachem Begin*, p. 203.

Chapter 6

22. Jehan Sadat, *A Woman of Egypt*. New York, Simon and Schuster, 1987, p. 75.
23. Anwar Sadat, *In Search of Identity*, p. 107.
24. Haber, *Menachem Begin*, p. 234.
25. Ibid.
26. Eric Silver, *Begin: The Haunted Prophet*, New York: Random House, 1984, p. 118.
27. Haber, *Menachem Begin*, p. 239.
28. Ibid., p. 244.

Chapter 7

29. Anwar Sadat, *In Search of Identity*, p. 150.
30. Ibid., p. 181.
31. Ibid., p. 204.
32. Perlmutter, *The Life and Times of Menachem Begin*, p. 289.
33. Quoted in Perlmutter, *The Life and Times of Menachem Begin*, p. 292.
34. Sullivan, *Sadat*, p. 66.
35. Jehan Sadat, *A Woman of Egypt*, pp. 254–255.
36. Anwar Sadat, *In Search of Identity*, p. 231.
37. Sullivan, *Sadat*, p. 99.

38. Anwar Sadat, *In Search of Identity*, p. 305.
39. Ibid., p. 306.
40. Haber, *Menachem Begin*, p. 8.

Chapter 8

41. Ibid., p. 1.
42. Anwar Sadat, *In Search of Identity*, p. 309.
43. Kenneth W. Stein, *Heroic Diplomacy*. New York: Routledge, 1999, p. 226.
44. Ibid., p. 227.
45. Sullivan, *Sadat*, p. 106.
46. Sadat, *In Search of Identity*, p. 311.
47. Perlmutter, *The Life and Times of Menachem Begin*, p. 337.
48. Stein, *Heroic Diplomacy*, p. 253
49. "The Nobel Peace Prize 1978: Presentation Speech." Available at www.nobelprize.org.
50. Ibid.
51. Silver, *Begin*, p. 206.
52. Ibid., p. 207.
53. "Anwar al-Sadat: Nobel Lecture." Available at www.nobelprize.org.

54. "Menachem Begin: Nobel Lecture." Available at www.nobelprize.org.

Chapter 9

55. Perlmutter, *The Life and Times of Menachem Begin*, p. 361.
56. Ibid., p. 362.
57. Sullivan, *Sadat*, p. 115.
58. Jehan Sadat, *A Woman of Egypt*, p. 433.
59. Ibid., p. 434.
60. Ibid., p. 28.
61. The BBC. Available at www.bbc.co.uk.
62. Ibid.
63. Jehan Sadat, *A Woman of Egypt*, p. 31.
64. Silver, *Begin*, p. 233.
65. Quoted in Ibid., p. 238.
66. Quoted in Ibid., p. 243.
67. Quoted in Ibid., pp. 251–252.
68. Anwar Sadat: Chair for Peace and Development. Available at http://www.bsos.umd.edu/sadat/.
69. Quoted in Anwar Sadat, *In Search of Identity*, p. 332.

"American Experience: Jimmy Carter." PBS Online. Available online. URL: http://www.pbs.org/wgbh/amex/carter/.

———. *White Nights: The Story of a Prisoner in Russia.* New York: Harper & Row, 1977.

The Egyptian Presidency. Available online. URL: http://www.presidency.gov.eg.

Haber, Eitan. *Menachem Begin.* New York: Delacorte, 1978.

Heikal, Mohammed. *Autumn of Fury.* New York: Random House, 1983.

Parker, Richard B., ed. *The October War: A Retrospective.* Gainesville: University Press of Florida, 2001.

Perlmutter, Amos. *The Life and Times of Menachem Begin.* Garden City, N.Y.: Doubleday, 1987.

Quandt, William B. *Camp David: Peacemaking and Politics.* Washington, D.C.: The Brookings Institution, 1986.

Rabinovich, Abraham. *The Yom Kippur War.* New York: Schocken Books, 2004.

Saunders, Harold H. *The Other Walls: The Politics of the Arab-Israeli Peace Process.* Washington, D.C.: American Enterprise Institute for Public Policy Research, 1985.

Silver, Eric. *Begin: The Haunted Prophet.* New York: Random House, 1984.

"Special Report: Egypt." Guardian Unlimited. Available online. URL: http://www.guardian.co.uk/egypt/.

Stein, Kenneth W. *Heroic Diplomacy: Sadat, Kissinger, Carter, Begin, and the Quest for Arab-Israeli Peace.* New York: Routledge, 1999.

Sullivan, George. *Sadat.* New York: Walker, 1981.

FURTHER READING

Books

Begin, Menachem. *The Revolt.* New York: Nash, 1977.

———. *White Nights: The Story of a Prisoner in Russia.* New York: Harper & Row, 1977.

Carter, Jimmy. *Keeping Faith: Memoirs of a President.* New York: Bantam, 1982.

Fromkin, David. *A Peace to End All Peace.* New York: Avon, 1989.

Lewis, Bernard. *The Middle East.* New York: Scribner, 1997.

Sadat, Anwar. *In Search of Identity.* New York: Harper & Row, 1977.

Sadat, Jehan. *A Woman of Egypt.* New York: Simon & Schuster, 1987.

Web sites

Anwar Sadat: Chair for Peace and Development
http://www.bsos.umd.edu/sadat/

Britannica Guide to the Nobel Prizes
http://www.britannica.com/nobel

The Carter Center
http://www.cartercenter.org

Israel Ministry of Foreign Affairs
http://www.israel-mfa.gov.il

Jewish Virtual Library, "Menachem Begin"
http://www.jewishvirtuallibrary.org/jsource/biography/begin.html

The Menachem Begin Heritage Foundation
http://www.begincenter.org.il

Nobelprize.org
http://www.nobelprize.org

The Washington Institute for Near East Policy
http://www.washingtoninstitute.org

PICTURE CREDITS

ABOUT THE AUTHOR

HEATHER LEHR WAGNER is a writer and editor. She is the author of more than 30 books that explore social and political issues and focus on the lives of prominent men and women. She earned a B.A. in political science from Duke University and an M.A. in government from the College of William and Mary. She lives with her husband and family in Pennsylvania. She is the author of *Henry Kissinger, Elie Wiesel,* and *Rigoberta Menchú Tum* in the MODERN PEACEMAKERS series.